GLIMPSES OF THE MIDDLE EAST

Lady Patience Moberly was born in 1923. She was one of the first women to qualify as a doctor from St George's in London, after which she became a paediatrician. She later married a diplomat, John Moberly, and joined him in the Persian Gulf for their first posting as a married couple. She entered the sensitive but dangerous world of the Middle East: Iraq under Saddam Hussein, Jordan, Lebanon and Palestine. Permitted behind the curtain, she observed the lives of women and paints an empathetic picture of a deeply traditional society and a centuries-old way of life on the brink of dramatic change. The ambassador's wife knows everything, hears secrets, witnesses duplicity, but is not allowed to express a political opinion. Now, aged 93, she expresses her views plainly: the Iraq War was unnecessary and the plight of the Palestinians is appalling. John and Patience Moberly were responsible for starting and training the first Intensive Care Unit in Gaza, they were founding members of Medical Aid for Palestinians, MAP, and any proceeds from this book will go to that charity.

Glimpses of the Middle East

By Patience Moberly

Scotland Street Press
7/1 Scotland Street
Edinburgh EH3 6PP

ISBN: 978-1-910895-02-3

Typeset by Palimpsest Book Production Limited, Falkirk, Stirlingshire
Printed in Scotland by Bell & Bain Limited, Glasgow

Jacket artwork and design by Theodore Shack.
Back cover from a photograph of John and Patience Moberly.

TO JOHN IN MEMORY OF THE MANY
HAPPY TIMES WE HAD TOGETHER

QATAR

Two weeks after I was engaged, in 1959, my fiancé told me
he had been posted to Qatar as a Political Agent, starting in
eight weeks' time. I'd never heard of the place.

"How do you spell that?" I asked.

"Q.A.T.A.R."

"I suppose that is what I call Quetta."

But of course it wasn't, and eight weeks later we were
landing in Kuwait in August, en route to this Sheikhdom in
the Persian Gulf.

At that time in 1959 with their newly discovered oil, the Gulf
Sheikhdoms were both potentially excessively rich and at the
same time politically very vulnerable. Britain had a treaty
arrangement with them to protect them from outside attack
in exchange for conducting their foreign affairs, but the
running of their internal affairs was entirely independent. In
each Sheikhdom a British Foreign Office official called a
Political Agent oversaw this arrangement under the overall

guidance of a more senior diplomat in Bahrain called the Political Resident. The inhabitants of Qatar were, of course, mainly the Qataris themselves, ruled by their traditional Ruler, with a fairly large expatriate group consisting of Indian servants, professional Arabs and oil workers, the most senior of whom were predominantly British.

I got out of the plane that August day and looked around for the furnace which must clearly be nearby, because no climate could possibly be as hot as this. There was no furnace, it was just the Gulf on a nice cool summer evening. Twenty-four hours later we were staying in Bahrain for a night, before flying on to Qatar the next morning. Our kind Foreign Office host, standing in for his boss, the Political Resident, who was away at the time, had organised a supper party for us to meet various colleagues. I sat next to him and he began to talk about my husband's new job.

"There's a lot of unrest here at the moment," he said. "If you had real trouble I suppose we might be able to get you out. The Consul in Mosul was killed recently by the mob. Head split open with a pickaxe, like a rotten orange. I hope we could get you out in time." He obviously wasn't convinced he could. He talked on, thinking about the problem. I assumed he must be giving me an unofficial warning that my husband of three weeks would probably shortly be killed. Somehow I managed to get through that terrible supper which seemed to go on for ever, before we could go to bed. But how could I tell John it was likely he would soon be murdered? I waited till he was asleep, then put my head under the pillow and wept and wept.

The next morning in a little plane with the mail bags, a man in a dishdasha, and a goat, we set off on the last leg of our journey. I was quite certain I would shortly be returning as a widow.

We were met at the Doha airport by John's second in command, and there also seemed to be quite a crowd of people on the tarmac, who we supposed must be waiting for someone else. It turned out they too were part of our welcoming party.

"You'll love it here," they said, beaming. "So much better than stuffy old Bahrain."

It was the beginning of two and a half fascinating years in what was still a mediaeval Arab society. There were no mobs with pickaxes.

From the nightmare of the supposed danger to John to an almost fairy-tale meeting with the Sheikh was only a matter of hours. The Ruler's eldest son was giving a feast in our honour that evening. We drove out across the desert in the dark to a large fort-like building with turrets lit by neon lights and a huge door covered by an illuminated Qatari flag, like a scene from a Hollywood Arabian Nights. As we approached, the door was flung open and we were in a great courtyard filled with servants and retainers armed with guns and bayonets, dimly seen in the half-light. At another door on the other side the Sheikh, resplendent in his Arab robes, was waiting to greet us. We processed into a huge majlis, or reception room, carpeted in green with green velvet chairs round the walls and further chairs in the centre. It seemed all the rank and fashion of Qatar, both European and Arab, were there, nearly all men though with a few European women, who all came forward and shook John's hand. Then everyone relaxed onto chairs and talked and drank Arabic coffee. I found myself between my husband and a cheerful beady-eyed Sheikh who I tried but failed to talk to in Arabic. Fortunately, not talking is not considered rude, which is a marvellously restful convention.

After a while the Sheikh got up and we all walked across the courtyard to the banqueting hall, another huge room, this time decorated entirely in red – carpets, walls, curtains, even the chandeliers. There was the most enormous table I have ever seen, covered with more food than one would believe possible – plates and plates of goat meat, turkey, chicken, rice, vegetables, fruit and sweetmeats, as far as the eye could see. The Sheikh sat at the end with John and me on either side on gold and red velvet chairs. We were no sooner seated than a host of servants armed with knives fell upon the meat and started piling it onto our plates, which were soon so high with food there was no more room, and still they came. I was aghast, until I realised guests were not expected to eat everything, indeed it would be rude to do so; the thing they must never do is refuse. When a guest has finished he gets up and leaves, even if his host is still eating. A servant appears with a bowl and a golden jug of water, soap and a towel, for washing hands, then he wanders back to the majlis. In due course the Sheikh joined us, there was more coffee, and then it was time to go.

I had noticed, as we ate, a crowd of retainers at the open

4

door, watching proceedings with avid interest. This was the second eleven, waiting to dash in and take our places as soon as we left. They in turn would be followed by the third eleven, and so on down the pecking order. Finally, the remains of the feast were carried away on huge platters on the servants' heads to feed their families. So this great excess of food was eventually distributed to nearly everyone.

There would be many more meals of this sort during our stay in Qatar, though very few approaching this one in magnificence. Arabs regard hospitality and generosity as being of the utmost importance. From the highest to the lowest, they entertain their guest with immense courtesy and respect. Whereas in the Western world entertaining in one's own home across social barriers is not so common, in the Middle East no matter what these social differences may be, hospitality will be offered and received with great politeness and dignity. What might seem to us wasteful and ostentatious is in fact the height of good manners and is meant to indicate honour and respect for the guest.

The most enjoyable meals, though, were the simpler ones, sitting in a circle on the floor round a communal plate and eating with our hands, quite an art in itself. Traditionally, the food is always eaten with the right hand, never the left. When it comes to rice, it is pressed into a little ball in the palm of the hand and then flicked into the mouth with the thumb, which is also quite a skill. Arabic coffee is thin and highly spiced, and is always served in small cups without handles from a special coffee pot with a large beaked spout. The guest takes the cup in his right hand and drinks it, then holds it up to the coffee pourer, who fills it again. To drink one cup is mandatory, to drink three is a sign of appreciation and satisfaction, but it has to stop there. After the third cup it is held up and shaken and will then be taken away. There were tales of foreigners who did not know this and became desperate, as there appeared no way of stopping the flow. There were also dark tales from the past of the place this ritual had played in some Sheikhdoms with a disputed succession in the ruling family. The coffee could not be refused, and the taste of poison could be hidden by the strong coffee flavour. It was said one formidable mother gathered all her sons together and made them swear on the Quran they would not murder each other in this way.

Looking back on all the generous hospitality we received during our two and a half years in Qatar, it is perhaps ungracious to remember the one occasion when things did not go quite according to plan. This was not anything to do with the Qataris nor anything official, but a friendly invitation from two Syrian engineers we had got to know and had to lunch from time to time, feeling they were rather homesick for their families still in Syria. My parents were staying with us when they invited us all to lunch in a garden, just outside the town. This turned out to be a very attractive walled area full of shady palm trees and oleanders. Just inside the wall of the garden, when we arrived, we saw a blood-stained wooden crate covered with flies, which appeared to be our lunch. Our hosts lit a very small fire and fixed the lamb carcase, which they removed from the crate, onto a spit high above the flames, and we settled down to with drinks to await the meal. In what seemed a remarkably short time, lunch was declared ready and our plates were quickly piled with chunks of virtually raw meat, which was literally inedible.

"Eat up, eat up," said our kind hosts. "You are welcome, you are welcome."

What to do? To refuse the meat and to eat it were both impossible. We could not let our friends, who had gone to so much trouble and expense, realise our dilemma. But my mother was a keen gardener.

"Come and look at these interesting oleanders," I said. We walked off exclaiming and pointing at these very common plants, quickly followed by my father and my husband, who had also developed a sudden intense interest in horticulture. Before long our plates were cleared and we could happily return to our hosts.

"Oh, but your plates are empty," said our hospitable friends, seizing them and piling them high again for another go.

It was expected that I would visit, at any rate, the chief wives of the Ruler and his family, and also some of the wives of the chief merchants. In the case of the Ruler's wives, all of them lived in separate houses, which were pleasant villas in walled gardens. One would be met by a male servant and taken to the women's quarters, to be greeted there by the Sheikha and her companions. Usually they were very friendly and welcoming, though one discovered there were many subtle nuances of behaviour depending on where exactly they met one. All of the Ruler's ladies would be masked in the betulah, which covered their faces from forehead to chin, with only their very made-up eyes visible, the shiny black masks pleated over the nose giving the effect of a flock of beautiful perfumed crows as they advanced. They wore long filmy dresses worn over brightly coloured trousers tight at the ankle, with a diaphanous black shawl over their heads and usually a black gold-edged abba, or cloak, over all.

There was said to be a ceremony when a girl reached puberty, when her family saw her face for the last time. After this, for the rest of her, life she only took off her betulah when she was with her husband or when she prayed. Only once, when I went to visit a very senior and educated Sheikha who I knew fairly well, did I find to my astonishment she was unmasked. My knowledge of etiquette had not prepared me for such a situation and I did not know how I was expected to react, but fortunately her "lady in waiting" quickly solved the problem by asking "How do you find the Sheikha without her mask?"

I was able to reply truthfully that I thought she was very beautiful.

"Yes" was the rejoinder. "What a shame she has to cover her face like this, she has such a lovely big nose."

Sometimes there were so many people to greet one and shake hands that it was difficult to tell which of them was the Sheikha and which her mother or aunt or sister or cousin or servant, because they were all part of the family and all came and sat round on the floor, and listened and looked and talked. But the more senior ladies sat in the chairs round the side of the room, and the Sheikha herself would wear a great deal of wonderful jewellery and was often very dignified. It was a very relaxed atmosphere as people wandered in, talked, wandered out again, reappeared, talked to each other, said nothing, all with no intention of rudeness and no sense of strain. In the same way, the English visitor did not need to talk a great deal or could talk in English to a companion she might have come with, without causing offence.

Visitors were offered soft drinks and then great piles of fruit and sweetmeats and finally Arabic coffee, which was the signal that the visit was over and they were expected to leave. Since it would have been unpardonably rude to leave before the coffee was served, this situation could lead to difficulties. With a party of other European men and their wives, we were asked to lunch by a Sheikh who lived some way out in the desert. After the whole group had lunched with the men, we women asked if we could visit the ladies. These wives lived in an enclosed courtyard with no windows onto the outside world, not even a glimpse of the sea nearby. It was clear when we arrived that visitors were infrequent and probably they had never met a European before. They were very excited by us.

"Why were my eyes blue and not brown?"

"My country was cold and theirs was hot. So their eyes had to be stronger."

"But why was my country colder? How curious."

They talked and talked and asked innumerable questions. Time passed and eventually we had to ask if the coffee could be brought, as our husbands were waiting.

"Yes, yes. It was just coming." Nothing happened. Time passed. We tried again.

"Our husbands would be wanting to leave. We must go."
No result. Then:

"They would be angry with us."

"They would punish us when we got home." Finally in desperation:

"If we don't leave, now they will beat us."

Immediate fascinated attention.

"Do they beat you?"

"No, of course not. What about you?"

"Well, they used to beat us a lot. But now a good wife costs a lakh of rupees or more, they take much more care of us."

I was met with questions like this on other occasions. Some of them were fascinated by the idea that anyone could die of a bad heart. (A visiting nurse had just suggested this.)

"Could you really die of a bad heart? How extraordinary!"

It was explained the heart was like a pump, pumping blood around the body. Even more astonishing and interesting. Then they wanted to know why we were fair and they were dark, did the earth really go round the sun and, if so, how did it do it?

Of course this did not apply to the more senior wives, nor some of the more sophisticated ladies, particularly the non-Qatari wives of the merchants, who never wore the betulah and were only veiled when they went out, and at home were dressed in the height of revealing French fashion. They were less formal and seemed to spend most of their time, when it was not too hot, in cloistered tree-shaded courtyards with the whole "family", from the wife to the servant and her baby, gossiping or working.

Contrary to the belief of Westerners, many of them did not envy our freedom. We tended to be slim, which was a clear sign our husbands did not give us enough to eat.

"Come on. Eat up," said a jolly fat little Sheikha. "Then you will be nice and plump like me."

They heard some of us worked or went shopping in the Souk, which certainly meant our husbands were too mean to get enough servants, and the fact that we were not hung with jewels made it obvious they did not love us much. I got the impression that many of them were happy and content with all the family comings and goings. Certainly there were no sad lonely single women or neglected widows as there are in our society, and they were looked after from the cradle to the grave. As well as this, all the brothers, uncles, cousins and all the servants of both sexes were allowed in and out. With the telephone ringing constantly with the latest news, they were absolutely at the centre of things and what they didn't know about wasn't worth knowing. These ladies were clearly very important and powerful and, in some cases, were in fact running their husband's businesses. In one of the Sheikhdoms down the Gulf the Ruler conducted all his important meetings sitting in front of a large curtain. It was said his first wife, who was also his chief advisor, was seated behind the curtain, so that later on they could discuss these matters together.

One of the great fascinations of living for some time in an alien culture is to try to understand why these communities do what they do and have adopted practices and systems that often seem to us curious and, in some cases, profoundly wrong. The answers, I think, lie in their very different basic assumptions about life, and the very different environment in which they live. The most basic assumption of these traditional Arabs is that their family honour is of supreme and overriding importance. This is demonstrated in the modesty and chastity of their women, but the behaviour of the women is overseen and controlled by the men whose responsibility it is to enforce it. Inevitably, this implies that women will not be allowed the freedom to go out and about in the way Westerners do. Also society is more violent, and in that context women will always be vulnerable and in need of protection. Provided the women keep to the rules, they are in many ways better treated and safer than in Western societies, but if they step out of line they are in big trouble. However, human nature being what it is, power and influence, like water, find their own level, and there is more than one way of obtaining it, even or perhaps particularly, in a harem.

We had been in Qatar a little while when we were asked to lunch with one of the lesser Sheikhs, who lived a short way outside the town. A group of expatriates working, for example, in the Oil Companies and the Government, with their wives, were also guests. We all sat out on the shady roof of the house talking before the meal began. Suddenly our host began upbraiding my husband for treating me so badly. John was somewhat taken aback. By then we'd only been married about a year and he thought he was doing quite well, as indeed did I. What was he talking about?

"Look at all these men here," said our host gesturing at the other guests. "Mr. So and So of the Bank, he has an assistant. Mr. Such and Such of the Water Company, he has an assistant too." He went round the whole group. "All of them have assistants. Only your poor wife doesn't have one. It's not fair on her. You should do something about it."

We met this idea in another form a little later when a Muscati working in the Agency asked if he could have leave to return to Muscat to find a young girl to help his wife, who was struggling with a new baby. When after several weeks he came back and was asked how he had got on, he replied rather sheepishly, "Well, in the end I decided to marry another wife. So much cheaper." Quite a lot of men I met told me it was a very sensible plan and that the wives thought so too. But I never met a woman who liked the idea at all.

Though four wives are allowed to Muslim men, most of them did not have so many, and in the more advanced countries it was very unusual. After all, four wives is a big expense, and the husband is commanded by the Quran to treat them all exactly the same, though everyone admits it is difficult to dictate the feelings of the heart. In Qatar the first wife was, as is traditional, a cousin or close relative, and usually retained her position as first wife throughout her life. The second was the current favourite and often had a lot of influence. The third would be the ex-favourite and the fourth a very temporary young lady, who would be divorced and sent home after a few months, no doubt with many presents and jewels and with no impediment to marrying again. The husband could divorce his wife by saying three times "I divorce you." It was also possible, though much more difficult, for the wife to divorce her husband, the real problem in her case being that custody of the children was almost always given to the man, so she would lose them if she did. The man had to pay what was sometimes referred to as the Bride Price to the woman's family before they married. However, often the money was only promised and not paid unless divorce was threatened, when it acted as a significant deterrent to marriage break-up and a kind of insurance for the wife, who would then return to her father's or her brother's house. Some people felt that over all this was in many ways a fairer method of dealing with the problem than pertained in those days in the West, with its culture, in many countries, of serial polygamy.

Fairly early on during our stay in Qatar my husband had to go on an expedition to the south of the country to confirm the border with Abu Dhabi. The party took with them three old men who were considered experts on exactly where the frontier had always been. For a time they stumped about the desert grazing grounds, showing where the tribes had traditionally fed their flocks. All went well until about half way through they suddenly decided the Ruler might prefer it if they moved the frontier several miles further on. When this adjustment had been firmly dealt with, a small tent was erected and everybody had lunch. Afterwards the oldest and most notorious of the three started boasting of his success as a slave trader.

"The mother of Prince So and So, I found her and sold her

to Ibn Saud. And the mother of Sheik Such and Such, it was I who brought her to the Ruler."

There was not the slightest understanding that anyone could consider this in any way wrong.

Slavery had been abolished in Qatar ten years earlier. Up to that time slaves had been sold in the Souk and it was still said that any slave who grasped the Agency flag pole could demand and be granted his freedom, though this never happened in my husband's time. Most of the domestic servants were really slaves, and one of the most powerful men in Doha was the Ruler's Chief Slave, who was reputed to be a millionaire, owned several houses and was feared by many people. I also met on one occasion a prosperous and apparently contented wife of one of the leading merchants, who had been captured in Abu Dhabi as a girl and sold to the man who eventually became her husband. Had that not happened, she might well have had a life of extreme poverty and certainly no more freedom than she now had.

It is interesting that none of the founders of the great monotheistic religions condemned slavery, which has been the universal practice underpinning almost all the great civilisations of the world. Again, perhaps in a violent and lawless society, the poor and powerless do better under the protection of a powerful person, however wrong and unjust it seems to us.

One morning my husband was sitting in his office when the Chief of Police entered the room and flung something across his desk.

"What do you think of that?" he said as the bundle unrolled and revealed a blood-stained shirt wrapped around a blood-stained knife. The shirt belonged to the much respected senior surgeon of the Government Hospital, Dr. MacCrae. The story was that Dr. MacCrae had recently removed the appendix of a Yemeni, who, as was to be expected, suffered a certain amount of post-operative pain. The patient felt the correct reaction to this was to seek revenge. As soon as he could, he left the hospital, went to the Souk, bought a large knife and returned, intent on killing a doctor. As luck would have it, just as he entered the foyer Dr. MacCrae was posting a letter there. He plunged the knife into the Doctor's back, narrowly missing his main artery, and withdrew it to have another go, when fortunately the Doctor's cries brought friends to the rescue. Though the Doctor was very shocked, no lasting harm was done.

I had hoped to continue my profession as a paediatrician here, but it seemed there were some problems for people practising medicine. It was decided it would be wiser if I saw only expatriate children, mainly European and some Indian or Arab, but not Qatari because of the possibility of political complications.

There were three hospitals in the Sheikhdom at that time. The Oil Company had a hospital at Umm Said, run by British doctors and mostly British nurses, which was for Oil Company employees, though at times they generously accepted others not in the Company.

The Government Hospital in Doha was the main hospital. I was allowed to admit patients there, though it was seldom necessary. Mostly I did domiciliary visits. I also spent a few days there on one occasion as a patient. It was comfortable, luxurious and rather disorganised. Every room had en suite facilities, but in many cases the plumbing didn't work and the room had not been cleaned. Most of the nurses were Indians, the ward sisters were Anglo-Indians or English and the Matron was English. A host of people seemed to flow in and out of my room – a man to clean the floor, another one to clean the lavatory, a lady in flowing robes and a betulah to clean a tiny spot off the window, another lady to clean another spot, a third lady to do the same thing, and then the first one again. (They were of course using cleaning as an excuse to see who I was, being insatiably curious.) From time to time I would look up and find the door half open and a pyramid of masked faces from the tallest lady to the smallest child gazing over each other's shoulders in fascination at this strange sight. Fortunately I discovered the door had a lock!

With my first breakfast I started to pour out my coffee, only to find it was just hot water. The trouble having been explained to a helpful attendant, another jug was brought, but again it was only water. A third helpful man appeared, entirely understood the situation and carried everything away, never to be seen again. That night as I lay in the dark dozing off to sleep, I was alarmed to realise there was a man in the room groping his way round my bed. Just another helpful person bringing a drink and not wishing to wake the patient.

More difficult was the fact that though I had been given a nice room, the air conditioner did not work and it was stiflingly hot. At first it was said the air conditioner was working. Then it was admitted it wasn't but that "A fan is very good". Finally it was agreed the AC did indeed need mending, but it couldn't be tonight and tomorrow was Friday, but on Saturday, God willing, something might be done. Fortunately at that moment my husband arrived, and within ten minutes I was in a lovely new room with two working air conditioners and a view.

The third hospital was a women's hospital for Qatari women, and mostly for maternity cases. It was run by a formidable Egyptian lady gynaecologist, who was a great favourite of the Sheikhas and therefore very powerful. It was said she had once been failed in a medical exam by an Egyptian professor, who later on was invited on an official visit to Qatar. She took her revenge by locking him in the lavatory, from which he finally escaped by climbing out of the window. She also had a grudge against the British Matron at the Government Hospital, and one day sent two of her female staff to remove her physically from her office. But the Matron was a tough lady and, during the tussle that ensued, seated herself in a large chair and held on so tightly that eventually her assailants had to leave defeated.

I was told this hospital was chaotic, with all the husbands allowed in the maternity ward all the time, many of them with their hawks on their wrists and with no concept of any sort of disciplined behaviour. But I never visited it, as it seemed a wise policy to be involved professionally only with expatriates. As a result, I only learned about many of the details of their lives and illnesses second hand. For instance, I was told sexual abuse of boys was very common, but very rare with girls, perhaps because of the premium put on female virginity. I also learned it was the practice in many parts of Arabia at that time to pack the birth canal of a recently delivered woman with salt, so as to hasten healing and enable her to return more quickly to her husband. The result of this was to produce increasing scarring and contractures with complications in subsequent labours and in some cases obstruction and death. I have no evidence that this took place in the women's hospital but it was certainly thought to be quite common in the population, as I believe I had occasion to observe.

One morning, whilst I was having breakfast on the roof of our house, I became aware of a series of increasingly loud shrieks coming from a large courtyard across the alleyway from our flat, which was situated in the old part of the town with Arab houses and courtyards all around us. Obviously it was not etiquette to stare into one's neighbour's backyard but with discretion it was possible to see what was going on. The cries came from a small single-storey house in the courtyard, and a little crowd was grouped round the door peering in. Very soon a taxi drew up in a great hurry and a very agitated older couple, who looked like parents, jumped out and rushed into the house. The cries continued in a crescendo, then there was one final shriek, followed by a dreadful silence. In a short while two white-coated doctors emerged, shaking their heads, and later that day a shrouded corpse was carried out on a bier. The most likely cause of this tragic event must surely have been that the poor lady was in obstructed labour and died of a ruptured uterus. Her two teenage daughters became greatly disturbed, wandering about the street in a way no respectable girl in that society would dream of doing. They must have felt like rats in a trap, with no possibility of avoiding marriage or repeated pregnancies, nor of shutting their eyes to the horrific dangers these might bring. Until that time I had sometimes wondered if, in spite of all our so-called advances, the Western culture was really of any benefit to this very traditional and stable society, but after this incident I had no doubts.

A few months after we arrived in Qatar, I came across a group of boys shouting and throwing stones under one of the parked cars nearby. There was a dog, little more than a puppy, under the car and they seemed to be intent on killing it. I shooed them off, rescued the dog and took it up to our flat. Fortunately, she was not hurt, only very frightened, and soon responded to kindness and food. She was a short-haired black and white mongrel who I called Mish mish (Arabic for "apricot") because of the colour of her brown ears. Inevitably, I felt I must keep her. This was not a very practical idea, but at first seemed to work quite well. She was almost but not quite house- trained. There had to be some discreet moving of furniture in John's study on one occasion to disguise an unfortunate stain on the carpet I could not wash out. After consultation with the local vet to ensure this would not in any way be a health hazard, I used to take her out in the back of my car when I went on my paediatric medical rounds, to the intense delight of my patients, who, if they were very good and not seriously ill, were allowed to see her at the end of the visit – a great boost to doctor-patient relationships. But of course like all dogs she had to be run every day, and inevitably was far too excited by the local smells to want to come back when we called her. There came a moment when John, the most accommodating of men, was stumping about the beach, declaring forcefully he could not spend all his time waiting around for the bloody dog, which was only too true, as an official engagement that evening was getting closer and closer. So Mish mish had to go. I missed her, but she found an ecstatic welcome with one of my expatriate patients.

On the whole the illnesses I saw were very similar to those I had encountered in England, with an added group of children with tropical diseases. The difference seemed to be, though this was only an impression rather than an established fact, that those who got ill seemed to be more severely affected and to deteriorate more quickly than would be expected at home. The hospitals at that time were not equipped to cope with very ill or complicated cases, so the situation could arise that the patient should be quickly evacuated home. This involved a long flight and very often would only be possible once a week. The dilemma, therefore, was whether it was safe to wait a week in the hope of improvement or whether by that time the patient would be too ill to be moved. One such case occurred with a lovely little fair-skinned blonde child, a sort of snow maiden, daughter of an English father and his beautiful Scandinavian wife. She became ill, rapidly deteriorated and clearly needed repatriation fast. A plane was sent to take her and her mother to Bahrain, where just in time they caught the commercial flight to London. When they arrived at Heathrow, her mother very understandably wanted to take her on to Scandinavia to be with her own family, and the doctor at the airport agreed to this. But as they approached Helsinki, the child suddenly collapsed and stopped breathing, and was only resuscitated in the nick of time. Eventually she made a complete recovery, but her case underlined the difficult and dangerous decisions that sometimes had to be made.

During our three years in Qatar, two people became very important in our lives and both became firm friends. The first we met the moment we entered our new flat when we arrived in Doha. We approached our home up a small dusty side street near the centre of the town. Beside the door to the flat an emaciated cow was eating a cardboard box by an open drain. Behind it, the door to the flat hung drunkenly on broken hinges. We mounted two long flights of stairs between peeling white walls ("like a run-down Peabody Buildings", as someone described it) to a doorway in which stood a resplendent white-haired figure with a smiling Indian face, dressed in the whitest of white starched uniforms with gleaming brass buttons. This was Piris, our butler, who was rapidly to become my right-hand man and our trusted friend. A Goan Christian, he had been in this post for many years and really ran the house. Everything I know about entertaining I learned by watching him. He was a superb organiser, and I always felt that if he had been born into another society and country, he would surely have become an important national figure, even perhaps a prime minister. When we planned parties or visits together, he knew everything about the local community and their foibles.

"Is the Chief of the Police coming, Madam? Then we can't

have prawns, they don't agree with him. Mrs. So and So particularly likes that sweet." Even more vital was his experience of organising the annual national day celebrations, always rather quaintly referred to as the Queen's Birthday Party.

"We will need so many bottles of wine, whisky, gin, soft drinks, extra glasses, plates, jugs, buckets of ice, extra waiters, etc., etc. and I will arrange." Which he did.

Our flat had been universally condemned for European occupation but was thought eminently suitable for HMG's representative. It was very drab and dowdy when we arrived but we managed to smarten it up with new paint and curtains, cleaned up the roof and used that as a reception area, with lovely views over the harbour and the Arab town, for big events. There was a rumour that the roof might collapse if we had too many guests, and that people stood around the edges where they felt it was safer, but fortunately there were no signs of any problems and the party went with a swing. Piris and I, discussing it all next day, felt it had been a success, and his post mortem of the event included not only exactly what had been consumed but also by whom.

"Mr. X, Madam, drank thirteen bottles of beer, and Mrs. Y, you know, the fat lady, she drank two thirds of a bottle of gin." There was a certain wicked amusement when one met these pillars of society later, remembering that bottle of gin, as well as a timely reminder that everything anyone did in this goldfish-bowl society was known and remembered.

As well as Piris, we had a cook and a sweeper called Ali. Every morning I used to watch Ali sweeping along the passage.

One morning I saw, to my surprise, that he had apparently, like an amoeba, split and there were two of him busy side by side, the only difference being that Ali Mark Two was a little thinner and shorter than Ali Mark One. I said nothing and waited for an explanation. It appeared that Ali Mark One was going on holiday and had arranged for his cousin to take his place, and was busy teaching him what he had to do.

This large number of staff might have been thought rather excessive for two people, but in fact we ran a small hotel. Until our last year, Qatar had no hotel, so an enormous number of official guests stayed with us, unless they could wangle an invitation from the head of the Qatar Petroleum Company, who provided much more luxurious accommodation. We had an average of two official guests every three days throughout the year, not to mention any family or friends who might come and see us, and literally hundreds of guests for meals, so good domestic back-up was essential. It was tiring, of course, but interesting, and in those three years we only had one really tiresome visitor, a large booming business man who tried his best to take over John's office the moment he arrived and had to be firmly dealt with.

Piris became the linchpin of our household, a benign dignified presence, always equable, reliable and helpful. Occasionally he would tell us tales of his time with his previous employer, an Indian rajah, and of the celebrations at his palace.

"And at midnight they clapped their hands and said 'Bring on the dancing girls,' and even the sweepers only drank champagne."

He spoke of the British Raj too. "In those days, Madam, when the people saw even the hat of the British District Officer, they trembled."

But I think the thing I most often remember about him was at the end of our time in Qatar. My husband became seriously ill and we moved him down to the Oil Company hospital twenty miles outside Doha. I stayed in the company rest house adjacent to the hospital. His condition rapidly deteriorated, until tt became more and more unlikely he would recover. After about a week he was flown home, desperately ill, and only by a miracle survived. During the agonising days before he was evacuated, whilst he was in the company hospital, one of the oil managers came once to see me, but apart from this no one else from the big British community surrounding the hospital visited me, and I was left quite alone. When Piris heard what had happened, his immediate reaction was "Oh, if only I had known, I would have come at once to keep you company."

When we left, things were so desperate we could not say goodbye properly to Piris. He had decided to retire and already had his ticket to Goa booked. After many extremely anxious weeks, John's condition improved and I tried to get in touch with Piris again, but no one could give me his address or tell me how to contact him. We both felt sure he would have wanted to be in touch and feared he must have died. I shall always think of him with great affection.

The other important person in our lives was Sifat, the Pathan driver. In theory, the official car was the property of HMG, but it was immediately apparent that in the sight of

God or Allah it belonged to Sifat. It was a Humber, the only one in the Sheikhdom, and the only one apart from the Ruler's cars to fly a flag on official occasions. It was Sifat's pride and joy, his baby, and the symbol of his status as a Great Man in the community. Every morning, whilst we were eating our breakfast on the roof of our flat, watching the white sailed dhows like a crowd of butterflies on the pale blue sea coming in to land their cargo in the harbour, Sifat was busy below, polishing and caring for his beloved vehicle. No matter how late we returned at night, it was always carefully tucked away in the garage before he went home. Sifat had been the official driver for a number of years and was one of the world's great enthusiasts. He hugely enjoyed being part of any local event, the grander the better. Official photographs of such occasions invariably featured his smiling brown face just behind the VIP who was taking part in the event. He knew everything and everybody, and had a special network of friends who could be relied on to solve almost any domestic problem. The most important of these would be described as "Very-Good- Men", and were usually Pathans or spoke Pushtu or had some other special virtue. If something needed mending or making, "my friend in the Souk" would appear and fix it. When we needed flowers (very difficult to get in that climate) to decorate the flat for the Queen's Birthday Party, "my friend will bring some", and large fronds of palms and real roses would miraculously appear, to decorate the long staircase up to our flat. I think it might have been a serious matter if Sifat did not like you.

"Oh, what a pity I not there," he said, hearing of a mugger

who attacked one of the Europeans in his house one evening. He joined his hands and twisted his wrists. "If I there, he dead, he sleep." But if he liked you, he was your friend for life.

He loved children. I imagine he greatly missed his own family in the North West Frontier. He was the only person I know who could pick up a baby he didn't know before and get an immediate smiling response. The older children loved him and were even sometimes allowed to "help" him clean the car, the ultimate sign of approval.

So Sifat became a great ally and an important part of our life, and all went well until he returned from his biannual leave, considerably later than he should but with the most convincing of excuses to explain his absence. Whilst he was away, a new expatriate manager, Mr. Thompson, had arrived in Qatar, and he had a Humber. It was bad enough there were now two of them, but the real disaster was that his was a shiny, very new model, which put Sifat's car in the shade. Worse was to come. One of our stream of visitors had to be entertained over the Friday "weekend". We had fairly unsophisticated amusements in those days and decided to take him to the Zoo. It was a small place, made with prodigious effort out of a patch of desert, with some parched grass in the centre and animal cages all around. I fear it was not the highlight of our guest's visit, but the rest of us enjoyed it, particularly Sifat.

"Oh, Memsahib, here is animal neck TOO long. Here is bird, maybe big chicken, maybe come from South America."

We gazed at the giraffes, ostriches and lions, and at the

oryx which was looking so lugubrious he might have known he was on the endangered species list. Then it was time to go home, but something was wrong with the car. It responded very sluggishly and we could see black smoke coming out of its exhaust. The next day it was rushed into the garage – the only garage in the Sheikhdom, which everyone went to – and the Very-Good-Man, Sifat's friend, of course, diagnosed it needed a new part, which he did not have himself, nor could it be found in any of the garages of the neighbouring Sheikhdoms, like Bahrain. It would have to be ordered from England. Urgent telegrams were sent and the new part arrived and was put into the car. We set out in the Humber the next day on the long drive to one of the oil camps seventy miles away on the coast, where we had been invited to a party, but the car was no better. We crept along with black smoke trailing behind us. And soon saw in the distance Mr. Thompson in his new car approaching at speed. He passed us with a wave of the hand and dwindled to a speck on the road ahead. We arrived late, Sifat was mercilessly teased by the other drivers and Mr. Thompson made some remark to John to the effect that it was not surprising our car was so slow considering it was so very old.

In the garage next day the Very-Good-Man admitted with the deepest shame he had made a mistake, he was very very sorry, he now realised it was a different spare part that was needed. But this part was even harder to get hold of. Even London could not supply one. It was very unlikely HMG would agree to a new car. Were we stuck with this old wreck for ever? For a week or so Sifat was sunk in the deepest gloom. He hardly smiled, though gradually he became more optimistic, "perhaps his friend could still do something after all". He took the car in again, watched over it lovingly all day and appeared the next day to take us down to the oil town twenty miles away on the other coast to another VIP reception. We set off early at our shamefully slow pace, and inevitably after a while saw Mr. Thompson speeding closer and closer behind.

"Poor old Sifat," we thought. "Another humiliation."

Then just as we were about to be overtaken, Sifat stepped on the accelerator and our car leapt forward. We roared ahead at over seventy miles an hour. Mr. Thompson was left a dwindling speck on the road, but this time far behind us. Sifat almost exploded with excitement.

"My friend very clever man," he said. "My car better now."

John asked him what he had done, got a rather vague answer and, perhaps wisely, did not press for details. Mr. Thompson was late and there were no more comments about the age of our car.

The next day, being driven round the Souk by Sifat, I asked again what had happened. There was a pause and I could see he was wrestling with a dilemma, whether to let me in on a huge joke or whether discretion was wiser. Fortunately, the joke won.

"Memsahib, what could I do? We needed this spare part. But we could not get it, not from London, not here, not anywhere. We had to have it. My car was very bad . . . But Mr. Thompson, he has a new Humber and it has to be serviced. And now perhaps his car has black smoke. My car is quite all right."

Some time after we left, Sifat retired. Last heard of, he was said to be living "in great content" in his mountain village, still, I am sure, enjoying every moment.

One of the most interesting characteristics of people in the Middle East is their almost infinite capacity to believe in conspiracy theories. So universal is this that we found that, if we invented the most bizarre and far-fetched explanation for any happening, we could be pretty sure it would be what the Arab Street would be saying. "If only," said my husband, "the British were half as clever and devious as the Arab world believes, we would have no trouble at all in the Middle East."

A typical case in point was when a bomb was placed in the British Bank of the Middle East in Doha during our stay in Qatar. The bomb went off and caused a little damage but fortunately no one was hurt. The rumours were rife, the front runner being that John had planted it there in order to produce unrest in the Sheikhdom, so that he could ask for British troops to be sent in, and give HMG an excuse to occupy the country. I was recounting this story with amusement to the sophisticated Manager of the Syrian Bank two or three days later.

"I did hear that," he said, looking extremely embarrassed, "but I said it could NOT be true." He clearly believed every word of it. I did not tell him the next favourite idea was that he, along with the managers of the other local banks, had been responsible. The thought of these three eminently respectable and serious middle-aged men creeping along at dead of night with their lethal weapon was particularly appealing. It later turned out the Omani Rebels were in fact the culprits.

A little later we had the chance to visit Oman, thanks to the kindness of the head of the Qatar Petroleum Company who was a friend of ours and was flying down with his small son on a company visit. We all boarded the small plane at the airport and, as always, I was pleased to see our pilot was an obviously competent and reliable Scot. Off we went and started taxiing along the runway.

"Daddy, the wing's on fire," said the small boy sitting across the aisle from me. Looking out, I did indeed see smoke and possibly a small flame coming from the wing on that side. Someone had told me people on these planes often mistakenly thought there was a fire on board. Not to worry. The plane gathered speed as we sped along the runway, added extra power for lift-off and, just as we were about to become airborne, came to a very sudden juddering stop. Even more alarmingly, the cockpit door flew open and our calm and reliable Scottish pilot, with a chalk-white face, dashed out shouting, "Get out of here as quick as you can!"

Somehow we got the emergency door open, jumped onto the sand below, and scuttled away from the plane as quickly as we could. What seemed a long while later, the airport fire engine and ambulance lumbered up to our aid. It appeared some vital bit of the engine had fallen off, the wing was being sprayed with fuel and, had we been just airborne, it could not have been put out. It would certainly have been a disaster. As the Oil Company chaplain said lugubriously later, "Another two seconds and I should have had a very sad duty to perform!"

We waited in the airport for a replacement plane to arrive and set off again about two hours later, having by then had enough time to take in just what a close shave it had been. Before long, we were flying over what was said to be the largest quicksand in the world, mile upon mile, as far as the eye could see, an ocean of scabrous evil-looking sand. Then the plane inched its way over the bare and jagged range of the Jebal Akhdar and we thankfully descended to the plain below.

It is very seldom one has the chance to see a truly mediaeval city, not only in its layout but in the life of its people. Muscat was such a place. The town was enclosed in an encircling wall pierced by three gates. – a small one for pedestrians and donkeys, a main one for ordinary traffic and a bigger one for larger traffic, which was only allowed in by special permission. Three hours after sunset, the main gate was closed and only opened the next morning. Anyone walking in the town after this, including the nightly street patrol, had to carry a lantern. In the morning, the gate was opened again and water was carried into the town in sheepskin containers carried on workmen's heads. There was no car park, but a camel park instead. From the town you can see the Old Portuguese Fort just off shore, a very picturesque building but a place of ill repute because the treatment of the Sultan's prisoners, shackled and held in its depths, was said to be terrible, part of the dark side of mediaeval life. At that time the Sultan had absolute power and ruled entirely as only he wished, apparently impervious to any new ideas.

All this has changed since then. Qatar too has altered greatly since we knew it. Our great good fortune was to have seen the Gulf before all these changes happened.

LEBANON

The Middle East Centre for Arabic Studies, MECAS for short, was the Foreign Office Arabic language school in the village of Shemlan, high up in the hills overlooking Beirut. In 1973 my husband, who had been a pupil there in previous years, was appointed Director of the school and we moved to Lebanon.

The position of Shemlan could not have been more beautiful. From the terraced garden of our house, the orchard and olive-clad slopes of the mountain fell away steeply to the coastal plain thousands of feet below, with Beirut in the distance on one side and on the other the sea curving up to the horizon, so that you could hardly tell where the water ended and the sky began. From our God's-eye view of the landscape we could watch the storm clouds rolling in to the land whilst we remained in sunshine, and at night the lights of Beirut twinkled in the distance echoing the stars above.

In spring the mountains were covered with flowers, and the many mountain birds were joined by flocks of migrating storks beating their way up the spine of the mountains to their summer breeding grounds in Asia Minor and the Balkans. I remember vividly a group of bee eaters, some of the most beautiful birds of the country, flashing red and gold and purple, that settled on our garden fence one morning, singing to each other with a haunting lilting song.

"In ten minutes," I said, "a little boy with a gun will come and shoot them." Which he did, only in five minutes not ten. A parable of Lebanon perhaps.

The students in the school followed a punishing schedule, initially for a year, at the end of which they could read, write and speak classical Arabic and were fluent in colloquial Arabic, in this case Lebanese. Some went on for a further six months to a higher exam and had by that time reached approximately the standard of an official interpreter. With this went a wide-ranging introduction to Middle East life and culture, with visiting experts in many fields coming to lecture at the Centre. It provided an invaluable, almost essential, skill for anyone working in the Middle East and attracted students of many different nationalities, not only British.

At first Lebanon seemed both beautiful and peaceful, and I was surprised when the British Ambassador, Sir Paul Wright, said to me soon after our arrival, "The whole place is on a knife edge. It is going to explode any minute. I keep telling them that but they won't listen."

The months passed and nothing seemed to happen, and I wondered in my ignorance why such an astute and clever man would be so pessimistic; but he was quite right, of course.

Under the surface the tensions were rising. Quite early on, a very Westernised, highly educated teacher in the school was inveighing against one of the other communities in the country.

"If they go on like this," he said, "we'll have to deal with them."

"What do you mean? Shoot them? Surely," I objected, "you don't really mean you would kill them? All of them? Their women and children? Surely not."

"Oh yes, we might have to" was the chilling reply.

But at first in our mountain fastness our chief interest was to get to know the village, which played an important part in the whole enterprise. Some of the students lived in the school itself, but many others were billeted on families in the village. The village arranged parties and social gatherings for them so they were quickly integrated into local life. Most of the villagers knew a great deal about how the course was run and how far advanced a particular student had progressed, and would tailor their vocabulary accordingly, or in some cases refuse to be bothered with them until they had reached a certain level of competence.

It was obviously important to get to know the people in the community as soon as possible, which in my case particularly meant the village women. And the first of those that I met was Rosa, who cleaned my house and told me her life story. To look at, she might have been an elderly English Rose, grey-haired, with very bright blue eyes and a very rosy complexion.

Rosa was the daughter of a single mother, who put her in

a convent the moment she was born, presumably because she was illegitimate. For three years she was looked after by one of the nuns, who obviously loved her and who Rosa adored. Then at the age of three she was taken away from the only "mother" she had ever known and put into domestic service. She was so small they had put a box for her to stand on in front of the sink, which otherwise she could not reach. All her life she had worked as a domestic and now was expected to look after the ill and very demanding mother who had treated her so badly. It was not uncommon to see young children working, though not, I am glad to say, as young as Rosa had been. Even the wife of a leading Beiruti paediatrician complained that the trouble with the little girl she employed was that she would try to play with her daughter's dolls.

But, apart from Rosa, how was I quickly to get to know the formidable matriarchs of the community who were, as in all villages, very important figures? I decided to invite them to an English tea party, but clearly in groups, as the numbers would otherwise be too big. Who should be asked first? It would be disastrous to get the protocol wrong. With help from the head of the church sorority, a series of lists of ladies in order of local importance was produced and I waited with some trepidation for the first group to arrive.

Exactly on time on the appointed day, a formidable army of the village matriarchs came marching up the hill, all in their best tight black outfits, their grey hair drawn back in immaculate buns. The students and teachers in the school which they passed on their way were said to be deeply impressed, not to say alarmed, by the sight, and indeed so was I. But everyone likes to talk about themselves, and they were all descended from just three families who had settled there a hundred years before to work in the silk mills, so I hoped it would be interesting for everyone to help make a village family tree. Armed with a large notice board, yellow and red drawing pins, and cotton to indicate marriages, all of them were soon talking and helping and, it appeared, enjoying themselves, so the ice was broken and we soon got to know each other. Interestingly enough, the Sociology Department of the American University of Beirut later became very interested in this because no one up to then had made a family tree involving all the women as well as the men.

Shemlan was a Maronite, that is a Christian, village, and some time later the wife of the Chief Instructor and I were asked to join the annual ladies' pilgrimage. We were seen off on the bus early in the morning by all the men, clearly worried and deeply suspicious of what we would get up to when we were no longer under their eye, though partly reassured by the presence of Abuna Yusef (Our Father Yusef), the priest who was in charge of the party. We got to our first stop, a well-known shrine high up in the mountain, and paid our devotions dutifully and sincerely. But after that everyone relaxed, the chitchat increased, the noise level swelled and it was quite clear they were all delighted to be off on their own for once without being supervised by the men. We stopped at little places of interest, ate our sandwich lunch at an attractive coffee house in a village in the hills and went on high into the mountains with lovely views. There was a final pit stop in a remote village before we turned for home. By this time everyone was singing, clapping, and the younger ones dancing the dabkhi (Lebanon's national dance) in the aisle of the bus. Several miles along the road someone suddenly cried out "Wain Abuna?" ("Where is our Father?") Horrors! He wasn't on the bus. We'd left him behind. The bus turned round hastily and we sped back along the way we had come. After quite a few miles, we saw still far off a stout and very angry figure stumping along the road towards us. He clambered in and gave us all a furious lecture for at least five minutes, ending with the final insult, "You're all Arabs, all of you." Everyone did their best to look suitably contrite, but it didn't stop the singing and the dancing until we finally arrived home, rather tired, to be greeted by a crowd of worried and rather disapproving men.

A little later there was a sadder village event. The nice man who owned the local café died, and we all went to pay our condolences. The men of the village, all in their best clothes, were seated on the ground floor, whilst all the women went up to a large room on the first floor, where a great crowd of them were seated round the walls, with the dead man dressed in his best suit lying on a bier in the centre. He was surrounded by his close female relatives, including, of course, his wife. She was expected to keep up a continuous wailing and weeping and embracing of the corpse, indeed not to do so would indicate she did not love him. It is the custom for burials to take place within 24 hours of death, but only the men go to the burial. I wondered if this made it more difficult for the women to accept the death, or if perhaps the obligatory outpouring of hysterical emotion forced upon them was cathartic, and helpful to the grieving process.

After the burial, the widow and her family receive condolence visits for a period of 40 days. It is an absolute obligation for friends and neighbours to visit them, and makes it much easier than in our society to know how the bereaved should be treated, and also gives a wise and accepted time scale in which the family can get used to their loss.

When I was learning Arabic in Lebanon, my tutor, a man, was at pains to make me translate a series of exercises, one of which was an account of the differences between Arab and Western women. It seemed the latter were shallow selfish creatures, only interested in amusing themselves, having a good time and thinking about their personal appearance. They were far too lazy and self-centred to have many, or any, children and only thought about their own good. In contrast, the Arab women were quiet, modest and self-sacrificing. They readily gave up their own wishes and comforts to have large families, entirely motivated by the good of the family. Though it was added that, once a woman had produced a child, she was treated with great honour and respect by everyone, particularly if the child was a boy. This somewhat inconsistent view was mirrored in other beliefs about family life at that time. It was not uncommon to meet people, mostly men, in those days, who declared a woman made no contribution to her unborn infant except to act as a seed bed to nurture him. At the same time, if a marriage didn't produce a son, it was of course the woman's fault, and some wives were divorced because of this.

Even highly educated men, including Europeans and Americans, often believed this and had never heard of the Y chromosome or the fact that only males can produce males. This ignorance of basic genetics meant that there was a lot of justification of the habit of arranging marriages between first cousins. It was felt to increase the stability of marriages. As one man said to me, "If I go astray, the irate father-in-law I have to cope with is also my uncle."

As for the risk of producing children with genetic defects, quite a lot of men denied it happened. The idea was that these damaged children would not live to reproduce, so there was no problem. I asked the American Professor of Genetics at the A.U.B. what he thought of this idea. He laughed. "Why do they think I am here then?" he said.

The girls were much more educated and open-minded about these ideas. I met quite a lot of young women who were very much against marrying a cousin and were fighting hard not to do it, but in those days it was quite an uphill struggle.

Apart from the interest of village life, so foreign yet also so similar to villages in England, there were endless other interests and people to get to know. Lebanon is a fascinating and beautiful country to explore. There are endless archaeological sites to visit and wonderful scenery. You can ski in winter and bathe in the sea in summer; indeed, if you want to, you can do both on the same day. It is a place full of history and variety and, of course, there is Beirut.

Beirut was surely the most exciting capital in the Middle

East, with a host of clever unusual people, theatres, concerts, museums, famous night clubs, and a frenetic social life summed up for me by a lady I met one evening:

"Oh how wonderful to see you again! Where have you been? We keep on talking about you, we have missed you so much. We keep on asking where you are. What did you say your name was?" It was also a place of deviousness, corruption and literally murderous politics. On one occasion in Beirut I met a man who was very anxious to know what my husband did.

"He's Principal of MECAS."

"Of MECAS?

"The Middle East Centre for Arabic Studies."

He looked blank.

"The British Arabic Language School up in the mountains in Shemlan."

He was still puzzled. The temptation was too great.

"You know," I said "the Spy School."

He was electrified. He did indeed know all about the Spy School. It was a notorious institution up in the mountains where the devious and perfidious British taught espionage to a series of young men, who were made to work extremely hard and from time to time were sent out into the neighbouring countries with books and codes to infiltrate the local population. There was a shooting range on the roof of the building, which students were seen entering, followed by loud reports and cries, and the notorious double agent Philby had been a student there. But what could my remark mean? Why had I said that? Was it because it was true? Or perhaps a bluff?

Or a double bluff or even a triple bluff? With carefully concealed wicked amusement I watched these thoughts flitting across his face, and knew he would be wondering about it for days.

Sadly for the conspiracy theorists, it was not a spy school, not least because it had students from numerous different countries, which would have made it impossible. The expeditions armed with codes were the language breaks undertaken near the end of the course, the shooting range was the squash court and Philby had never been a student there. Having said which, I have to admit the double agent Blake was there (and was said by his fellow students to be "the nicest person you could ever meet").

On the top of our house was a siren. If we were attacked, our village friends, who all had rifles and other weapons, promised us they would immediatelycome to our aid. It was no doubt a kind and friendly gesture but we both agreed it would be incredibly dangerous. But why should we be attacked? The situation was that in that part of the country there were many mountain villages, nearly all of different faiths, so that intermarriage was uncommon and there was very little communication between them. When tensions arose all the men took down their guns and started to patrol their perimeter and, of course, were likely to meet the next-door neighbours doing the same, with potentially dire results.

Underneath the surface the tensions were rising. Fairly soon after our arrival, a British couple living on the mountain not far from the school were found sitting in their garden murdered with bullet wounds in their heads. It was thought to be a contract killing, probably by the Israelis, and the rumours were that they were gun runners.

After this, the friend of a man we knew was passing a mountain villa in his car when it was stopped and he was forced into the back room of the house, where he found two other men were being held. The three of them were stood up against a wall. One of his captors shot the man on his left, then the man on his right, and was just about to shoot him when the leader of the gang wandered into the room, holding his papers, to announce that it was a mistake and he should be let go.

Gradually, these incidents of kidnap and murder increased. There came a moment when the school Administrator got a call from his wife, who had gone down to a friend's house one evening to play Scrabble. The call didn't really make sense and was almost immediately cut off. He immediately suspected something was very wrong, alerted my husband, who instantly told the police, then set off at once with him for the house. As they pulled up in front of it, four men with Kalashnikovs leapt out of the ditch and marched them at gunpoint into the house, where, sure enough, the wives were being held by more gunmen. Diplomacy has its uses. After a lot of talk, the intruders left with no one having been harmed, but taking a lot of equipment with them. When the coast was completely clear, the local police arrived in force, to demonstrate how courageous and efficient they had been.

This same lady had a further very unnerving experience. One afternoon her husband was away from home on business.

As it was blisteringly hot, she stripped, showered and lay down on the bed naked to cool off, with her back to the door, and fell asleep. She was woken by the sound of a man's footsteps coming along the passage towards her room. Her husband was away, there was no one else in the house and no one else had a key. She heard the man enter the room and forced herself to breathe slowly, not move, and pretend she was asleep. For a long time he stood there looking at her, then finally left. She never found out who he was.

The worst moment for our family was one afternoon when our six-year-old daughter and a friend were being driven up from the English School in the plain below. They came and went every day in a taxi, travelling a steep road with numerous hairpin bends, as it climbed up the mountain. We knew exactly when and where they would be on this road every afternoon and one day, just as they would have reached the middle of it, an Israeli jet zipped over the mountain, dived down and rocketed the road. For several agonising minutes we waited for them, until miraculously they appeared coming up towards us, not unduly worried, because the Druze taxi driver had pretended it was nothing to worry about. In fact, had they been a moment later, they would certainly have been killed.

As the situation got wors, the village got more and more agitated. We could see the flashes of gunfire and hear the sound of explosions in Beirut far below, with the increasing political unrest. At one point a new government was elected and the village celebrated with a *feu de joie*, but two days later this government fell and another group, who they feared, had taken over. The next morning, when I went shopping, I found everyone in despair.

"We know what will happen," they said. "All the foreigners will leave and the Eastern Bloc countries will come in, and we will all be massacred, as we were in the twenties."

It sounded hysterical at first, until one realised they had indeed been massacred within living memory, and had only too vivid memories of a past that we with our safe comfortable history could hardly imagine. And only a few years ahead, a series of grisly murders designed to make them leave would make the village a deserted empty shell.

In April 1975 two serious incidents of killing between the rival factions precipitated the beginning of the Lebanese Civil War. We had by then been told we were to be posted to Jordan, and left the country a few weeks later.

Fifteen years after this, I revisited Shemlan. Walid, a Druz, drove me there. This was now Druze country, so it was safe for him to come, but he had never visited Shemlan before.

"Is this the way?" he said. "Do you remember?"

Although we had lived there, the way up to the school was almost unrecognisable. It was so battered there was hardly any surface left and the weeds were encroaching so fast it had ceased to be a proper road at all.

"Let's try it," I said. He swung the car up and round and suddenly we were there, the long low building of the language school straight above us and, higher still, the Director's house, which had been our home for three years. The school was a dead building, with sightless eyes staring out across the hillside. The entrance door still stood, pockmarked with many bullet holes. Inside the place had been gutted – no window frames, no doors, no lights, no railings on the balconies, the big downstairs room empty and echoing, the classrooms full of rubble. Outside were pools of broken glass on the ground and one old shoe. And the vines were tumbling down the hillside, reaching out green fingers as if they would feed on its carcase. The steps up to our old house were almost covered with shrubs, and the garden, so lovingly tended, was a jungle. It was all very still, with one bird singing.

The place seemed frozen in time, but there were ghosts everywhere. Just below audible sound, the students talked and laughed, and the teachers murmured as they gossiped in between lessons in the passage. At the door Nassib, the Druze porter, stood watchfully. In the big reception room the village elders, with faces as gnarled as the olive trees they tended, listened with intense concentration to see if the Director would make one slip in grammar or pronunciation in his welcome speech in classical Arabic. So many memories and voices, they almost crowded out what Walid was saying.

"Why did you fight, Walid?" I asked.

He frowned, knitting his brows together, thinking hard. "We believed it was what we should do. We wanted our rights and there was no other way. I still think it was the right thing."

On the steep hillside below us, the ruins of the village stood silent. No one was left, everyone had fled years ago. Elias Tabib at the shop, who spoke very slowly using simple words so that the newest of the students could understand. Samir

Hitti, the butcher who never bothered with anyone until they had reached the Advanced Course. Father Yusef, fighting his valiant but unequal battle to control the formidable ladies of the village. The young girls, dressed in the latest fashion, sauntering down the street in their high heels, but always with a brother or cousin just behind, making sure they do not step out of line.

"My brother, my youngest brother, was fighting," said Walid. "I went to join him. I was beside him when he was wounded. I carried him in my arms to the emergency station. After such a short time the doctors came out. 'We are so sorry,' they said, 'there was nothing we could do.' He was my brother, my child, my son. For a whole year I was out of my mind."

Elias' cousin was dead, murdered in his shop. The two old people at the bottom of the village who thought their age would protect them were killed in their beds; and many more. And all the rest scattered like dust in the wind. Gone were the village evenings, with the table laid with Lebanese food, the wine and the coffee. The talk on the terraces under the shade of the vines, the click of worry beads.

"Welcome, welcome. Our house is your house."

"How are you? Please God, well."

"How is your health?"

"We thank God."

"We thought it would only last a year," said Walid, "but we fought for eight years and in the end we have gained nothing. Everything for us is just as it was before."

Beyond the skeletal ruined houses, thousands of feet below

us, the sea curved up to the horizon, so that you could not tell where it ended and the sky started, as it always did. It was very quiet. Even the bird was silent.

JORDAN

We were posted to Jordan a few weeks after the start of the Lebanese Civil War, and we drove to the frontier. As we started walking up to the Jordanian customs house, a smartly dressed young man came hurrying down the steps with hands outstretched.

"Welcome, Excellencies!" he said. I looked over my shoulder to see what notable VIP had been following us, then realised with amusement there was no one else there. In Jordan at that time foreign ambassadors called the King "Sir", the King called ambassadors "Sir" and "Excellencies" were two a penny.

We had reached that point in John's career when we inherited a house, as opposed to taking pot luck with what was locally available. It was a lovely house with a swimming pool and a garden, which became my pride and joy.

With the garden came Ahmed, the gardener, who I nicknamed "Ahmed-death-to-plants" because of his unfailing ability to destroy any really precious plant I had asked him to be particularly careful of. He taught me something about the Middle East that I should have learned long before. On one occasion I asked him to do something he was obviously very unwilling to do. After a lot of resistance he finally agreed. "Yes, Lady, I will do it."

I felt rather pleased I had managed to win this battle, but nothing happened. It finally dawned on me that his "Yes, Lady" actually meant "No, I won't". It is so rude to refuse openly in the Middle East that people just have to realise that on some occasions yes is in fact a polite no.

With the garden it seemed I also inherited a Jordanian neighbour, who after about nine months suddenly rang me up out of the blue, said she was longing to meet me, must come and see me as soon as possible, this week perhaps, the moment it could be arranged. Rather bemused, I of course asked her round and she quickly arrived with a bevy of young women that she introduced as daughters, daughters-in-law and other family members, and who were all carrying scissors. As soon as they had had coffee, she revealed that she had, they all had, an urgent need of bay leaves from the bush in my garden and had come to collect some. Fortunately the bush was large and healthy so, though they attacked it with great energy, it survived. Finally, armed with their spoils, they departed as quickly as they had come and I never saw them again.

We also inherited a cook and another house servant, who were both extremely dishonest. We were told the cook boasted about the amount of money he made each month by cheating the Ambassador. (It was said later on he set up a restaurant on the proceeds.) They had all sorts of ingenious ways of doing this, with for instance such tricks as substituting water for gin in bottles at parties, which could not be detected by looking at the bottles, and knowing the guests would be too polite to reveal to their hosts what had happened. When we had got rid of them, we appointed the third, and very young, man in the household to become top man in the house, a post which he held for many years with great efficiency and integrity, becoming a Great Man in his community and a lasting friend of all his employers. He was a Palestinian, and his great dream was to save enough money to buy a little farm in Palestine and retire there, but alas I fear he is still waiting.

Another inheritance was the two guards who were detailed to escort my husband to work. The theory was they all went off in the official car and changed the route they took every day. From our house to the Embassy was down a long straight road and it was not very practical advice, but in any case John had no intention of going in a car as he liked the morning walk. He was a fast walker and strode out briskly whilst the two guards, both short and rather tubby men, panted along some way behind, finding it quite difficult to keep up. This was an innovation they did not like at all and it was not long before a delegation of them arrived to say they were really worried about the Ambassador's safety. It would be so much better, they all thought, if he did as had happened before and they all rode in the car. They might have been right about the safety aspect, but it had no effect on the morning walk, which continued as before.

A final inheritance which we thankfully avoided taking on was a large and very fierce guard dog called Druid. It had been assigned by HMG to sit under the Ambassador's desk in the office and put the fear of God into everyone who came to see him. Even Military Attachés, surely the bravest of men, never went to see the Ambassador without arming themselves with Danegeld in the form of large quantities of dog biscuits in their pockets. Fortunately, everyone seemed to feel this was carrying security too far, and Druid was shipped off to Tel Aviv, where I have no doubt he did very well for himself.

Jordan is surely one of the nicest Middle Eastern countries to be posted to. To start with, it has a reasonable climate, hot in summer, of course, but not the devastating humid heat of the Gulf. In the winter it can be quite cold and there may even be snow, which is looked upon as a great bonus, because more water is saved if this happens than can be if there is only torrential rain. The country round Amman reminded me of the Downs in England with ranges of smooth low hills, green in winter, and in spring and early summer covered with wonderful wild flowers like a rock garden. In places there are little valleys, sometimes with streams lined with oleanders and tamarisks, and further north orchards and pine woods. There had been a big forestry programme, and once a year all the Great and the Good of Amman were expected to turn out and plant trees. No one was expected to do anything so physical as to wield a pickaxe in the rocky soil, only to put the saplings in already prepared holes and shovel a little earth on them. It was a satisfactory thing to do and we all felt virtuous and that we were saving the environment, until I was told later that just over the hill little boys with herds of goats were waiting for us to leave before they drove their flocks into the new plantation for a nice feed. A lot of people felt the goats were the bane of the countryside, constantly spoken of as a vital part of the economy of poorer families, yet destroying almost everything green in their path.

Further south was spectacular desert scenery, with Wadi Rum, and finally the Gulf of Aqaba, with its fabulous coral reefs and wonderful snorkelling.

But, far more important than this, the Jordanians are delightful friendly people, most welcoming to foreigners, who they allow to join in their lives with a generosity that is remarkable. One of their most endearing traits is their sense of humour. There would be times when we would all be standing around being pompous on some official occasion and would suddenly realise our Jordanian colleagues behind their serious official faces were finding it just as amusing as we were.

Jordanian society is much more Westernised than many others in the Middle East. Though the less well-off tended to be conservative and to dress traditionally, there was no fundamentalist dress code or strict segregation of the sexes. The great majority of the population are Muslims, but it is a secular society and Christians can practice their religion without any hindrance. The middle and upper classes are open, sophisticated, and mostly dress like Westerners, though there was a tendency for some of the girls in the University to wear traditional Arab dress because, I was told, it was a such a practical way of solving the age-old feminine dilemma of "what shall I wear?", since nothing was revealed under the all-enveloping Arab robe. This made life much cheaper and simpler. In some ways I think their society must have been very similar to the descriptions we have of Edwardian England at the beginning of the 20th century. There were large close-knit extended families, always headed by men, with very powerful matriarchs in the background, who often seemed to have more control over domestic matters than we do,. I met a man on one occasion who was complaining bitterly about moving house shortly. When I asked him why he was moving he replied with a despairing shrug, "I don't want to move at all. But my wife insists. What can I do?"

Nearly all the men had had a higher education and were in business or professional jobs. Some, though fewer, women had been to University and also worked outside the home, with the immense advantage over Western women in a similar position that their child-care problems were shared by the extended family. In fact, this arrangement could be taken far too far in our eyes on some occasions, when the maternal grandmother, or worse still, the mother-in-law, insisted on taking over the control of the baby completely. The head of the family – either the father or the eldest son – was responsible for providing for single, widowed or divorced women and the elderly in the family, who would automatically be part of the family home. I once asked a Jordanian friend how this worked in practice, as we Europeans felt it would be difficult to live so close together without quarrelling.

"Oh but we do, we do," she said. "Indeed we do."

Underpinning this were very strict rules as to what was acceptable behaviour, some of which came as a great surprise to foreigners, particularly to foreign wives married to Jordanians. Many British girls in this position confessed how difficult it was to make these mixed marriages work, that it was only because they were determined to do so that they had succeeded and that all the concessions had to come from their side.

A very simple thing would be that the husband would think it quite normal to go out at night without his wife and it was absolutely unacceptable to ask what he was doing or object in any way. A more unusual example was when a highly educated American wife of a sophisticated Government official went with him to a party in the USA and everyone played charades. This aroused quite unexpected fury in her husband, on the grounds that she was making a spectacle of herself in public. Another problem affected a Jordanian friend of mine – a most respected late-middle-aged widow, who was much involved in some very useful charitable work, but had to give it up because her son, who had just returned from taking a university degree in England, would not allow her to use the only way of getting to meetings, which was by being given a lift by a man who was an old friend of the family. There is an Arab proverb that "when a man and a woman are alone in a room, the Devil is the third." This clearly applies to cars as well.

King Hussein was a small, impressive and very charismatic man. At the age of 15, he was standing beside his grandfather,

King Abdullah, when the King was assassinated. Two years later Hussein himself became King. The early years of his reign were troubled and a number of attempts were made to assassinate him too. One of the conspirators was executed, but the rest were gradually rehabilitated and brought back into public life, and given posts of trust and responsibility in his government; at least one became an ambassador. People waiting to see the King on official business would be surprised to find themselves in his majlis with, for instance, one of the arch-conspirators of a previous attempt on his life. This way of dealing with his opponents showed not only his magnanimity but also his wisdom, because the people treated in this way became devoted and trustworthy government servants. Unlike so many rulers in the area, he did not take revenge.

His court was much more informal than that of many other rulers in the Middle East, and tales came back from his entourage, who accompanied him to Tehran, of the contrast with the Shah of Persia. Apparently, in that court the etiquette was extremely strict and rigid. When the Shah was present, no one expressed any opinion except what they thought he would like to hear, and all the discussions were upbeat and optimistic but, the moment the Shah left, his entourage spoke openly of their deep worries and pessimism about the future. Apparently, when the Shah faced really serious trouble with the religious leaders, King Hussein immediately flew to see him and said to him, "Come on, you must go at once and face these mullahs and sort out the trouble. And I will come with you to support you."

"But," said Hussein, "the Shah would not go. And when I saw that, I knew he was finished."

It was typical of Hussein that when he was faced with trouble he would immediately go and talk to the people concerned and try to sort it out. That was one of the reasons he was so successful and appeared to command great respect and public support.

When he married his fourth wife, we were all summoned to the wedding festivities, which took the form of a great party in the garden of the Queen Mother's house. Of course, a great many people were thinking the same thing but not saying what they thought, though I did find myself in animated conversion with the Chilean Ambassador on the subject of Henry the Eighth. One of the guests, who appeared to be enjoying it all very much, was the King's British second wife, Muna. She and Hussein had originally met when they were both young, because of a mutual passion for go-karting. It had been universally accepted that because she was British her two sons would not be considered as possible heirs to the throne. They therefore had the great good fortune to be brought up as more or less ordinary people and had careers of their own. The eldest son Abdullah became a very successful soldier, until he was suddenly declared future king just before his father's death in 1999. Until that time, the King's younger brother, Prince Hassan, had for many years been considered the heir apparent, and had supported his brother in every way. The sudden change of plan was clearly a great shock to many people, but Prince Hassan, who is an academic with many long-term interests, is still working for his country, and his particular work in multi-faith understanding, especially between Muslims and Christians may well be one of the most important things anyone can do for the Middle East. Muna, having behaved with great discretion and good sense for many years, is now installed in Amman, in the honoured position of mother of the King.

King Hussein had trained at Sandhurst and there was a long history of Anglo- Jordanian co-operation and good relations between the two countries. The Duke and Duchess of Kent were visitors when we were there and were entertained by Hussein in his beach house in Aqaba. Amongst other things, Hussein took them on flights in his helicopter to places like Petra, piloted by himself. There were some who found all this a little alarming, considering how difficult it is said to be to be a helicopter pilot, especially in such wild and rocky terrain, and particularly since Hussein's third wife had recently died in a helicopter crash. Our only personal encounter with his helicopter was a moment during this visit, when we were sailing a small dinghy in rather too calm weather, became aware of a helicopter very close and, looking up, saw Hussein's grinning face just above us as he tried to blow some more wind into our sails.

One of the pleasures of having a stream of visitors to stay was the chance of taking them to some of the numerous archaeological sites in Jordan. Many had not heard of the Roman city of Jerash, which is close to Amman and one of the easiest to get to. I think quite a lot of them envisaged something small and rather dull when I suggested it. If so, I never disillusioned them as we drove there. There was a small, rather rocky path which took them to the top end of the ruins and was awkward enough to need all their attention till we got to the right place. Then I would tell them to turn round and look, and wait for the invariable gasp of amazement at what lay before them. We would be looking down on a huge circular forum ringed with tall pillars, from which a wide processional way lined by buildings and ruins ran away to the distant city limits. The slopes on either side of this were covered with ruins, some of them standing to quite a height, and when you went down onto the road, you could see the marks of cartwheels and chariots gouged into the stones. It never failed to convey vividly what a Roman city must have been like. You could almost imagine it in its bustling, important heyday.

Another impressive and much less well known historic site was Beaufort Castle, a Crusader castle on the border of Jordan and Israel. There had been a considerable amount of rocketing and other attacks there and there was a permanent army post, with the soldiers providing security as well as guides or minders for any visitors.

When we visited it, the nice young soldier assigned to look after us was very taken by our little fair-haired blue-eyed daughter. He started picking her a bunch of wild flowers which were growing on a kind of lawn lying between two walls, when suddenly there was a loud cry, and flowers and soldier disappeared from sight, followed immediately by an ominous thud from the depths of the earth. The supposed lawn was in fact the unsafe roof of a large colonnaded chamber one storey below. Much concerned, we hurried as quickly as we could down some stone steps and found him lying on the ground, rather shocked and groaning slightly, but to our great relief not seriously hurt. He was quickly helped away by a group of his amused fellow soldiers with assurances that they would look after him.

We were now left without a guide, but there was another party there as well as us. Their guide quickly took charge of the situation and told us to wait in a small room in the centre of the castle whilst he collected his group who would join us. As we waited, I looked around and saw an inviting doorway leading to somewhere dark and interesting. I was just about to step through it to investigate when fortunately the guide returned, seized me by the arm and pulled me back with loud cries of "No. No." Then he took a stone and threw it through the door. It was a full three seconds before we heard it hit the earth hundreds of feet below. As I learned then, these ruins are honeycombed with enormous underground cisterns, and in fact another visitor had recently fallen into one here and perished. This was underlined when we reached the room in which the Crusaders' prisoners were tried. The judges sat on stone benches around the circular wall and in the centre was what appeared to be a wellhead the mouth of which was blocked by a huge stone. If the prisoner was innocent, all was well, but if he was guilty, the stone was removed and he was dropped through the opening and never heard of again.

But, of course, the most famous and impressive archaeological site in Jordan is Petra, the "Rose Red City half as old as time", which was lost to the world for about 500 years. The Nabateans, a tribe of traders, built it and maintained it over many centuries but they were finally defeated and dispersed in the third century AD. From then on, its importance and finally knowledge of its existence was lost to everyone except a few Bedu who lived in it and feared if it were known about, their livelihood and dwellings would be threatened. Finally, in 1812 a young Swiss explorer called Burckhard, who had converted to Islam and could pass himself off as an Arab, heard a rumour of its existence and, to avoid raising the suspicions of the local tribesmen, pretended to be a holy man who had vowed to sacrifice at Aaron's Tomb, which was situated on a rocky outcrop that could be approached through the valley of Petra.

When we were in Jordan, though of course well known, it had still not been fully developed as a world-class tourist centre. The way in was only on foot or on some very thin dejected horses. The actual approach to the valley through a cleft in the mountains known as the Siq must be one of the most dramatic in the world. The further it goes, the narrower it becomes and the higher the rocky sides of the path rise. Finally, the sky is almost a slit hundreds of feet above and the passage is so narrow a tall man can touch both sides at once with his outstretched arms. Just as it seems it is going to close completely, there is a final opening and you see beyond it a beautiful pink building carved in a wall of rock facing you across a narrow space. You emerge into a glimmering pink valley awash with sunlight, which opens up to reveal further numerous pink buildings and tombs, as well as a Roman amphitheatre and street. At the far end of the valley, a stony path leads you up to a huge crenellated tomb (for some reason, always called the Monastery), from the top of which you get a wonderful view of mountains and valleys beyond. At the near end, a processional way leads up to the High Place, where on a flat area is a sacrificial altar, complete with a channel cut in the rock to catch the victim's blood. No doubt it was usually animals that were involved, but there is a contemporary account of a young man being sacrificed there too. It is so strange that the Nabateans, who were clearly very technically advanced with a remarkable drainage and water-collecting system and very fine pottery, should be so primitive in other ways.

In those days it was possible to get permission to camp in Petra. We did so at a moment when there had been a sudden rare fall of snow. The contrast of the snow on the pink rocks was stunning, but the night we spent in one of the caves was one of the coldest I had ever endured. The next day we followed Burckhard's footsteps to Aaron's Tomb. I was a bit doubtful about this part of the expedition, having a great dislike of heights, but a little boy with a donkey was coming with us as a guide and, where a donkey can go, surely a reluctant climber can venture too. Unfortunately, when we got to Aaron's Tomb, it turned out the lucky donkey had a snug stable at the base of this huge rocky pillar and the only way for the two-legged was on and up. The top, when we finally reached it, was a rather desolate place with a solitary bare Muslim tomb on it. By then, I had decided I could never get down the hair-raising path we had ascended and would have to spend the rest of my life up there with food somehow delivered by helicopter on a weekly basis. My mountaineering husband did somehow get us all down the outward sloping steps covered with ice, with the mist swirling round the rock clearing briefly from time to time to reveal the valley floor thousands of feet below. I was very pleased to see the donkey again.

When we finally got back to the Siq, I was reminded of a friend of mine who had come to Petra a little while before and taken a guide to show her round. On that occasion it rained a lot and she was amused and a little irritated at the fuss he made about this, and particularly about their return through the Siq. For a long time he stood about dithering, deciding what they should do, then finally made up his mind and said they would go "at once, quickly" and hurried her on her horse up the narrow path. Just before they emerged at the top, they met a party of about 20 French tourists with their priest, walking down the way they had come. A very short time later, a flash flood poured down the Siq and nearly all the unfortunate tourists were drowned.

But even more fascinating than these well-known ruins was the chance of exploring prehistoric sites far out in the desert. We teamed up with our American and French colleagues, usually guided by an American archaeologist who was working in Amman, and set off with large stocks of water, petrol, spare tyres and other vital supplies for two- or, very occasionally, three-day trips. The American Ambassador supplied radio contact with the outside world, the Frenchman supplied his best wine, which he maintained was wasted on official guests, and the three wives produced meals in rotation. There were no tents but everyone had a camp bed so we all slept well, and at night someone would produce a few logs so we could light a fire and sit round it.

There is a special magic about desert travel. You turn off the paved road onto the desert track, perhaps you skirt round a small hill or climb a gentle rise before the land falls away, and you head into a completely different world. Modern life is left behind; there is only this great space and emptiness, as if creation had just happened. The land lies before you, mile upon mile, fold upon fold, enormous and bare. You may find yourself skimming along the packed white mud of a dried-up lake or climbing gravel ridges and twisting down them like a giant roller coaster, or driving at speed through soft sand as if you are skiing. Sometimes there are low bushes or feathery tamarisk trees or, occasionally, great stretches of bare sand with huge outcrops of coloured rocks standing like sentinels. If you encounter sand dunes, which will always face the same way with a gentle slope on one side and a steep slope on the other, you climb up the gentle slope, pivot on the top edge and hopefully toboggan down the other side without turning over.

At midday the heat can be fearsome, as if an enormous pulsating oven was open, pouring heat at you. The air shimmers and throbs and the haze obscures the view or melts into mirages. But at night it cools down. With a full moon the whole landscape is flooded with brilliant silver light and, when the moon sets, the stars and shooting stars are so bright you could almost touch them.

We found many fascinating prehistoric sites – a Palaeolithic encampment littered with large hand axes, a flat area covered with offcuts from Stone Age tools, apparently a prehistoric tool-making factory, faint traces of an early Christian settlement and a hermitage, and, most remarkable of all, a rock carving of a prehistoric ox wounded by spears. Only on one occasion were there any worries about these journeys, when I woke in the middle of the night to find my little daughter standing by my bed under the starry sky saying she had a terrible pain and felt very ill. Initially, it sounded like appendicitis and for a short while we seemed to be facing the awful dilemma of whether to go back at once, eight hours' bumpy drive to Amman, or to go on another six-hour drive to a one-horse Saudi town with heaven knew what sort of medical facilities, if any, both options being very dangerous. What a relief when eventually it proved to be only the usual Middle Eastern tummy upset!

On our return journey on that occasion, when we were fortunately back on paved roads, we saw advancing towards us as far as the eye could see a towering wall of boiling black cloud. It was an approaching sand storm and, when it hit us, visibility was so bad we could hardly see the front of the car. No wonder if you meet one the only thing to do is, like the camels, try to get some shelter and wait for it to pass, even if it lasts for a day or more.

In Jordan for a while I joined a paediatric clinic run by some Roman Catholic nuns. It was very enjoyable because, almost uniquely in my experience in the Middle East, there was time to see the patients properly. One of the great problems the doctors often face is the great number of patients clamouring to be seen. Finally it becomes like a type of veterinary medicine and a self-perpetuating problem. Because there is no time to talk or explain to the patients, they feel worried and dissatisfied and seek another opinion, and then another and another, thus inflating their numbers many times, a vicious circle it is very difficult to deal with. When talking to mothers in the Middle East, there were sometimes differences of perception which to a European were difficult to understand. Very often if you asked a woman how many children she had, she would reply with the number of sons. Only if pressed would she volunteer the number of daughters and, if finally asked directly, would say if there had been any deaths, quite calmly, almost as if it didn't matter. European women usually find it very difficult to mention a child's death, even after many years, without obvious emotion. I cannot believe Middle Eastern mothers do not love their children just as much as Westerners do. Perhaps this stoicism is part of the fatalism of Middle Eastern philosophy, particularly of Islam, "It is God's will."

Do Middle Eastern parents discriminate in favour of boys? The mortality statistics suggest they do. The higher mortality amongst girls in some Middle Eastern countries is exactly the opposite of the findings in the West, where the slight majority of boy babies always born, and their higher death rate, leads to an even representation of the sexes at maturity. The only child patient I remember without a family member always by her bedside was a Kurdish girl of about twelve years old in the American University in Beirut. There was no one sitting with her. She was suffering from a particularly unpleasant cancer of her femur and was about to be sent home to die in a Beirut slum, where there was no palliative or other care. She clutched my hand as I passed.

"Oh, Doctor," she said, "I am so frightened, I am so frightened I am going to die." And the awful thing was I did not know any Kurdish and could not properly talk to her. I always wondered, if she had been a boy, whether she would have been left alone like that.

Hospitality, of course, is one of the key features of Middle Eastern culture. The classic Arab story of the role of hospitality is of the Sheikh who owned a wonderful horse, which was the envy of all who knew him and was greatly desired by all of them. One day an important visitor came to see him and was treated to a magnificent feast in his honour. After the meal the visitor broached the reason for his visit. He had come to see if his host would sell or give him the horse. The reply from the host was "You have just eaten it."

This exaggerated and wildly quixotic gesture has certainly brought fame and honour to its perpetrator, but I wonder if his motive was not so much to give help or pleasure to the guest but to increase his standing as a host. We were from time to time entertained by a rich merchant who always invited his guests for dinner at eight o'clock, but kept them drinking for three hours without food until the meal was finally served at eleven o'clock, followed quickly by coffee, at which point the exhausted guests could finally leave. It was thought he delayed the food so that they were forced to stay very late, which would indicate it had been a very successful party. It seemed to me that at the end of a long day our guests, particularly the men, were hungry and tired, and what they needed was to be fed and watered, and only after that would they be able to relax and enjoy themselves. So, rightly or wrongly, I started to bring the food and coffee on early, having explained this was not a plan to shorten the time they stayed but only intended to look after them better. Whether this was sensible or not I do not know. I was amused by the comment of my neighbour, the wife of the Iranian Ambassador: "Oh, we do all so enjoy your parties. We all come, and then we all go away again!"

In fact, in the Middle East entertaining is particularly necessary because personal contacts and friendships are considered of the utmost importance. The Western mode of rapidly changing executives and negotiators is far less successful. Great weight is put on dealing if possible with people who have been friends over many years, so that someone who has worked in a junior capacity in an Arab country and later returns in a very senior position may have very enviable contact with some of his old friends now amongst the most influential men in the country, to the great benefit of both sides.

One of the great perks of being an Ambassador in a country like Jordan is that he, and in many cases his wife, can probably meet all the interesting people in the country or visiting it. A busy VIP on an official visit will not spare time for Mr. and Mrs. Bloggs, but almost certainly will for HM Ambassador. By the same token, if there is anything interesting going on in the country, provided it is not a security issue, it is almost certain he can go and see it, be it an archaeological dig, an agricultural or industrial project, or a school, or, in Jordan, one of the many charities which flourish there. In the case of charities, one was often greeted by several important men who took one round, talking learnedly, followed by a group of women who said very little, but who one later discovered did all the work and really ran the organisation. I was surprised at the number of institutions dealing with orphans that we came across, but I discovered the children of the first wife may be classified as orphans if the husband marries again after her death.

Among the many remarkable charity workers we met, two people come vividly to mind. The monk, Father Andrew, a young man who with his staff lived in the most Spartan conditions in a large house in Salt, near Amman, running a pioneer School for the Deaf, a greatly needed charity helping what was at that time a largely unrecognised need. I often thought that those of us who met such dedicated workers were somehow inclined to feel that the harsh conditions and inevitable stress under which they worked was less difficult for them than it would be for us. But this surely this was not true at all and I admired them so much more because of this.

The other person was an English lady called Miss Coate, who spent the last week of her life in Jordan in our house, having fallen seriously ill and waiting to be flown home to England, where she subsequently died. She told me how she was in Jordan at the time of the great influx of Palestinian refugees and had realised that, though a lot of help was given to the women, there was no programme of help or support for the men, who were mostly small farmers, and were left with nothing to do, demoralised and despairing. She decided they needed land to cultivate, but the price of suitable land was prohibitive and she had very little money to dispose of. However, she found an area near a ruined castle in Zerka, which would have been very suitable, but had no access to any water and was therefore useless. In spite of the incredulity of everyone else, she bought it for a very low price, "Because," she said, "I knew there must have been water near the castle for them to do the washing." Then she brought in a water diviner and, against all the predictions of the experts, her belief was justified. There was indeed water there and she was able to settle a considerable number of Palestinian families very successfully, a notable triumph of stubborn practical common sense over the wisdom of the Wise.

Sooner or later, many people who stay in the Middle East get the feeling they ought to, just once, try to ride a camel. We had our Tourist Trap Camel Experience in the Wadi Rum, a marvellously dramatic area in the south of Jordan, where huge pink masses of limestone rock rise for hundreds of feet out of the flat desert floor. The trip we went on offered a camel ride along the Wadi, a night's stop in a Bedouin-style camp and a return camel journey the next day. It has to be said it is difficult for the newcomer to develop a very close affinity with a camel. Seen in the distance in a long line setting out on a desert journey, they look romantic enough. But at close quarters, for most of us there seems little hope of establishing a meaningful relationship, as one might, for instance, with a horse. A horse will look at you as you approach it, it will try to communicate with you in its own way, and there is a sporting chance it will do what you want it to. None of this is true of a camel. It doesn't really seem to see you with its hooded eyes. It has loose, almost prehensile lips, and slobbers greenish sputum, and groans and complains loudly whenever it is made to kneel down or rise up again, or indeed do anything. Above all, it is very loth to do what its rider wants, and being seated high up on its back on a not too comfortable saddle makes all this a rather surreal experience. The only way to direct it is either by hitting the side of its neck with a stick, or pulling on the rope of its halter to indicate a change of direction.

On this occasion, one of our party was our brother-in-law, who was a vet, and we felt sure he at least would be up to the challenge. But when he pulled the relevant rope, the camel's head moved fractionally to the left, but the camel itself kept walking resolutely ahead. A further pull and the same thing happened. Its head came further and further round but there was no change in direction. Finally it was looking straight backwards like a bird preening its tail, but still walking resolutely forward as before. Only when all the other camels veered to the left did it finally agree to follow suit.

The Bedouin camp was also not quite the experience we had hoped for, being chiefly notable for the extreme hardness of the ground and the loud snores of the rest of the party. In spite of all this, it was interesting to see a little more of what Bedouin life must be like, and how cleverly they adapt to this harsh climate. To Westerners, the complete lack of privacy in their life style would seem difficult, and explains their strict rules governing gender relationships and behaviour. I was also told by a lady anthropologist I met, who had lived several months with some Bedu, that for a lot of the time life was very dull, and the women might sit together evening after evening in complete silence because there was nothing to talk about. No wonder strangers tend to arouse such interest.

Another aspect of Bedu life which was surprising was told me by an older man who had once been a member of the Camel Corp, which had some oversight of their welfare. Though the Bedu were marvellously adapted to surviving in the searing summer heat, it was a different matter if there was a severe winter. He described how, following a really cold snap with a snow storm, they became worried about a Bedu family and went to search for them. They found them with the entire extended family sitting grouped in their tents round the ashes of a dead fire and all of them dead from cold. Many Bedu of today have become highly educated and successful in the modern world. They are much admired and people are proud to tell you they are of Bedu origin.

Not far from Wadi Rum is the Gulf of Aqaba and Jordan's seaside resort. It is a place of wonderful coral reefs. Snorkelling over them was like entering a fairy land of movement and colour. The shoals of brilliantly coloured fish, each seemingly more amazing and exotic than the last, were totally unafraid of the presence of humans swimming amongst them, and could be watched pursuing their busy lives all around one within touching distance, like a miniature God's-eye view of the Universe. There were only two fish to beware of – the Turkey Fish, which is a colourful, curiously encrusted creature with a very poisonous sting, and the Stone Fish, which lies on the sea bed pretending to be a stone and whose sting was said to be fatal. Fortunately, though we saw both of them, we had no occasion to find out if these reports were true.

Another less orthodox amusement was when we were staying with our children at the Aqaba Hotel during the week of a full moon. In the brilliant light of the moon the garden lay white before us, with the blackest of black shadows under the palm trees. You could stand or lie in these shadows and be virtually invisible to someone less than a foot away, having suddenly acquired almost magical properties of disappearance and reappearance. This turned a very ordinary game of hide and seek into something really exciting, which we all enjoyed immensely. I wondered what the staid guests eating their suppers in the hotel beside us thought of these goings-on just outside their windows, but in fact they never noticed.

One of my final memories of Jordan is the place where the river from the Wadi Mujib flows into the Dead Sea. It is approached by boat, or a gruelling walk over a steep rocky path, intensely hot in summer, which leads to a spit of land, where this seemingly miraculous cold freshwater river pours out of a cleft in the cliffs bordering the Sea. To us idle people who travelled by boat, it was a joy to watch the ecstatic expressions of the exhausted walkers as they arrived and plunged into its wonderful coolness. It was possible to wade and then swim up it, where the sides of the cleft became higher and higher and closer and closer together until, like the Siq in Petra, there remained only a sliver of sky far above. Finally, the river turned a corner and from the depth of a black cave it could be heard roaring over a waterfall as it emerged from its underground channel. To turn on one's back and float down it again, gazing up at the gigantic rocky walls and the thin line of sky was, an almost unbelievable experience never to be forgotten. It is so sad to hear that it no longer flows out of the ground like this because the precious water has been diverted upstream to supply the needs of the thirsty land.

IRAQ

To arrive in Baghdad during the Iran/Iraq War was like entering another planet. All flights were scheduled at night across endless black desert, to land in the blacked-out town. The airport was a forbidding palace of black marble, lit by thin crescentic roof lights. There was a drive on unlit roads and blacked-out streets to arrive finally at a dark empty house firmly locked, until eventually a drunken cook was hauled out of bed and produced a key. We woke the next morning to the sound of the muezzin, the bulbuls singing in the trees in the garden and the creak of a cart on the road outside. Welcome to Baghdad!

In previous times the British Embassy in Baghdad had been a palatial building in a large garden on the banks of the Tigris but, during the revolution in 1958, in which King Feisal was assassinated as well as his pro-British Prime Minister Nuri Said, the Embassy was attacked by the Baghdad mob and the Residency, apart from one large reception room, burnt down.

One of the Embassy staff was killed and the Ambassador and his wife made to stand for hours under the boiling July sun. The Embassy itself survived and continued to function as an office, but it was not surprising that the house in the suburbs now used by the Ambassador was not to be compared to the lovely house we had had in Amman. It was big and dark and unwelcoming.

I quickly discovered, talking to the other wives, that the greatest problem which affected us all was the lack of adequate cooling and heating in our houses. The climate of Baghdad is very extreme, with temperatures up to 160°F in the summer and below freezing in the winter. In summer the houses, in spite of being "cooled", were commonly up to at least 120° all day, and in winter remained obstinately at 50°, so that most of the Embassy staff, including ourselves, were living for a lot of the time in very uncomfortable conditions. Quite apart from this, a great many were housed in down-at-heel dilapidated old buildings, in many cases furnished with broken unusable furniture, which had been turned out by other posts in the Middle East. Everyone was amazingly positive and resilient but how could they be expected to continue content and healthy in such a situation?

I determined it would be my priority whilst we were there to try to ensure everyone had a house with at least two or three comfortable rooms in which to live and relax. The traditional Iraqi method of cooling was with air coolers in which water was run over a rotating drum of straw and by evaporation cooled the house. This worked well in medium heat but was useless when temperatures were really high.

Their added disadvantage was that they constantly went wrong, and tired husbands returning from the office had to spend long hours trying to get them to work again. It has seemed to me that the powers that be in the office in London were well aware of the problems of cold climates, but found it difficult to envisage the extreme discomfort of severe heat. At any rate, it was at first suggested the air coolers were not only perfectly adequate but in fact much healthier than efficient air conditioners. We quickly refuted this suggestion and asked them to explain why then it was essential for the staff in the Embassy to have air conditioners whilst they were not needed by the wives at home.

After we had been there a while, a trio of Government Inspectors arrived on a routine visit. By this time we were into the cold season. All the heating was done by small oil heaters. While giving out very little heat, they produced a strong smell of kerosene, which became nauseating after a time. In our house the temperature was on one occasion so low we had to go to bed to keep warm, and even then the Queen only gave us a single eiderdown for a double bed. The Inspectors worked in the Office and the lady of the party complained of being cold and asked for an extra heater. There were no extra heaters, but to our dismay the Counsellor nobly gave her his only one and shivered in chivalrous silence in his unheated room. We all felt he had sold the pass to the enemy. But the message got through. When they came to see us in the Residence we were, as always, dressed in our thickest ski clothes, and this was noted. Soon after, everyone was issued with efficient air conditioners, which doubled in the winter as efficient heaters, and life became much better for us all.

For us, there were a few relatively minor problems. The Battle of the Cockroaches, which I had anticipated downstairs in the kitchen, but felt a little unnerved about when I found a most enormous specimen plodding purposefully along the upstairs passage to our bedroom. The rats, upstairs and downstairs. The fungi growing luxuriantly on the rotting wood between the two kitchen sinks. And a plague of woolly bears, which are little black furry insects that live in soft furnishings and are very difficult to eradicate.

But one wonderful day the bare shrub outside our living-room window, which I had intended to cut down, suddenly burst into a blaze of beautiful orange flowers, the cold abated, and with spring coming on we could look forward to a few months of good weather and enjoy the Embassy swimming pool and tennis courts before the heat of summer started. For many months the Office's battles with the Treasury over decent houses seemed to be unending and sometimes despairing. However, two years later, just before we left, it was really gratifying when I asked around how people felt about their housing and the invariable reply now was they were "very nice and cool" and the houses were more or less adequate.

As soon as we stepped outside the house, the sentry at the gate started talking into his walkie-talkie, and as we walked up the street past other houses in this up-market residential suburb, other sentries outside other houses one after the other did the same. We walked along a pavement and were suddenly shouted at and pushed into the road by an irate man and, a little further on, our way was barred by a very hostile individual who would not let us pass. Very soon we discovered where we could go and where the demarcation lines were, and provided we kept to them there was no trouble, though one Embassy couple strayed by mistake into what would now be called the Green Zone and were both beaten up, even though the woman was pregnant. But everywhere we sensed the underlying violence, the men with guns who shouted and threatened anyone who stepped out of line, the ubiquitous white Mercedes driven by well-dressed armed men, who were the Mukhabarat, or Security Services. When my husband went to the barber, in contrast to every other Middle Eastern country, where the moment he sat down he would be bombarded with questions and chat, in Iraq the whole procedure was carried on in complete silence. When I went to the Souk, instead of the usual Middle Eastern smiles and friendly laughter at my poor Arabic, there was always an initial start of alarm, as they realised I was a foreigner, followed by monosyllabic replies or, again, silence. They appeared to regard us as a cross between criminals and lepers. Saddam Hussein had recently gone on the TV and announced that anyone who had anything to do with foreigners, particularly diplomats, would be considered a traitor. The fear was palpable.

In such a situation it seemed most unlikely I would be able to practise any sort of medicine, particularly because the medical establishment was in a state of shock over the fate of the previous MOH, as was described to me by a lady who was a friend of his wife. He was a member of the Revolutionary Council, which was discussing how to bring an end to the War. The Iranians had said they would never make peace whilst Saddam was in power.

"Then why don't you pretend to step down for three months?" suggested the Minister. "We will make peace, then you will return."

"That is a very interesting idea," replied Saddam.

He called a servant over and told him to put his hands on one of the stoves. In a few seconds the man was crying with pain. The Minister left instantly, rushed home and told his wife, "He means to burn me."

"You must escape at once," she said. He immediately jumped into his car and raced down the long road to Basra, but before he got there he had a traffic "accident" and was killed.

In spite of this, to our great surprise, when my husband wrote to the new MOH, he agreed I could visit and work in the Children's Hospital. I met the head of the hospital service and was introduced to an extremely pleasant consultant paediatrician, Dr. Rahim, who spoke perfect English and had trained in England, and had been assigned to look after me. I learned much later that all his colleagues were horrified, telling him he would be killed if he did so, and can only marvel at his courage at taking me on. We walked across the hospital courtyard to his office, which he shared with a colleague, who shortly arrived in the room. He was a very Westernised older man with a kind intelligent face, the sort of clever courteous doctor one would be only too happy to have in an illness. I was introduced, and his face became contorted with fury.

"What did you say your name was? What did you say your husband did?" he shouted, banging the table with his fist. "Why are you in my office? Why are you in my office?"

In vain we assured him my presence was officially approved and he would not get into trouble, before we hurriedly left. About a week later I met him doing a ward round.

"Oh Doctor, how nice to see you. Come and look at this interesting case." He had been reassured I was safe. More than anything else in Iraq, this incident brought home to me the terrible cloud of fear under which they all lived.

"What do you want to do in the hospital?" asked Dr. Rahim as we walked to the main hospital building.

"I thought I might do out-patient clinics," I said. I had done this in England and it would fit in well with my life here.

"I don't think you'll be able to," he said, "but we'll see."

How right he was! We went over to one of the clinic rooms in the Outpatients Department. Across the room facing us was a long plastic-covered bench and behind it a closed door. At a given moment the door opened and in burst three large ladies in black chadors, each holding a baby wailing loudly, who they dumped on their backs side by side on the bench and forced straight, like an open jack-knife. Behind them a mob of other mothers and fathers with their babies pressed in, all shouting at the tops of their voices, pushing forward X-rays, prescriptions and other papers, and all demanding attention at once. It was bedlam. In this clinic it was expected a doctor would see 100 cases a morning, an impossible task.

It was agreed I should go to the main hospital wards and work there.

I was to share an office with a delightful lady doctor called Leila. It was a very happy arrangement. She was an excellent paediatrician, pretty and petite, with whom I quickly discovered I had a great deal in common. From the clinical point of view, it was extremely interesting, since this was a tertiary referral hospital, with a very wide variety of cases, including illnesses now very rarely seen in the UK, such as diphtheria, tropical diseases, and a whole host of congenital and genetic diseases, which were a reflection of the frequency of consanguineous marriages.

It seemed the most useful thing I could do was to spend time taking medical histories and examining the children, the other doctors being so busy they had very little time either to do so or to think about their cases. Almost all the children in the wards would have an adoring granny sitting patiently by their bedside in their long robes and black headscarves day after day. I had only to appear, sit down, and ask in my halting Iraqi Arabic, "Aish bee? What is the matter?" and all the grannies converged talking as hard as they could, interjecting and adding information in an effort to help. My Arabic was more or less adequate to get the essentials. You don't need many words to take a medical history, but it was frustratingly inadequate in picking up all the asides and nuances which would have given such a fascinating insight into Iraqi family life.

However, in the secretive and enclosed world of Iraq, it was possible to get some idea about Iraqi society by talking to the younger doctors. No one could deny the cruelty and tyranny of Saddam's rule, but he had done great things for the treatment of women and for medical education. There were many more women doctors in senior posts working in the hospital than you would have found in the UK. The girls and boys were all educated similarly, and the top 10 % were allowed to choose whether to be doctors or engineers. (There was no bias against girls being engineers in Iraq.) The next 10 % were told which of these professions they must enter, and so on with other occupations down the academic scale. One of the house doctors really wanted to run a florist shop, but a doctor she had to be. After they had qualified, they were sent out to work in Government clinics in the countryside, often single-handed, and had to stay there several years before they were allowed back into the towns. It must have been hair-raising for the doctor and not very safe for the patients, but at least it was better than nothing, and was beginning to provide a nationwide primary health care service.

In spite of all this equality, though, there were still considerable barriers to the social mixing of the sexes. Some of the naughty girls took a wicked delight in jostling one of the registrars, who was a very serious and devout fundamentalist Shia with a black beard and an unfortunate irritating manner. They knew that any forbidden physical contact of this sort would mean he would have to spend a long time on his ablutions when he next went to pray, and made sure this would always happen. It was also interesting to observe everyone's behaviour at the weekly Grand Rounds, when all the staff met in the lecture theatre to discuss interesting cases. The young men sat on one side of the auditorium and the girls on the other. But I never saw in England such fluttering of eyelashes and covert glances from modestly cast-down eyes on one side, nor such flashing of eyes and twirling of moustaches as went on on the other side. Clearly, segregating the sexes has an emotional pressure-cooker effect.

Of course, I never mentioned politics whilst I was there, it would have been far too dangerous for the Iraqis. There were only two exceptions to this. One of the consultants, in good standing in the Baath Party, took me into his office one day, locked the door, and spent half an hour haranguing me on the situation. The gist of what he was saying was that yes, Saddam "did not have a kind heart", but he was all they'd got and "if we had anyone else, believe you me, they would be worse, they would be worse." During this conversation several people tried the door. I said to my husband later there would be only two explanations as to why it was locked, politics or sex, probably the latter. On the other occasion, one of the younger doctors suddenly burst out on a ward round, "This Devil's regime. I am forced to stay in this job. I cannot leave, even though I am paid so little I cannot even afford a car, let alone a house or a wife, and there is no way out."

"Don't say it, don't say it," we implored him, horrified at the danger he was putting himself in. I just hope no one reported him.

In Iraq at that time, while the qualifying degrees were taken in the country, postgraduates travelled abroad for further studies, and most of them spent some time in Britain and obtained British higher degrees. (Many of them also married British nurses.) In fact, at that time the greatest numbers of foreign students studying in Britain were Iraqis, and the standard of medicine was very high.

However, I encountered an interesting and surprising discrepancy in some undergraduates I was once asked to teach on the subject of congenital heart disease. They were all highly intelligent and well-trained young people and their knowledge of the different types of malformed hearts which might be encountered was excellent and detailed, much better than mine. But when I then asked why it was important to know about this, I was met with a complete blank. The simple idea that, if malformed, a pump like the heart might be inefficient or fail, with dire consequences to the patient, had apparently not entered their minds.

This confirmed what we had already noted in Palestine and what other Westerners teaching in the Middle East in different subjects have commented on, that traditionally there seems to be a much greater willingness to accept rote learning and authority than is found in the West. It has been suggested that this concept of unchanging and indisputable authority is more acceptable to Muslims because they all study the Quran, often learning it by heart, and the Quran cannot be altered or disputed in any way because they believe it to be the Word of God dictated to the Prophet, and therefore immutable. This might mean that the idea of criticism of authority was less comfortable for them than it is for us.

My general impression of the medicine in Iraq, which many others confirm, was that it was very good, probably some of the best in the Middle East, particularly in surgery and acute medicine. Where the system could not cope adequately was in dealing with the large numbers of very complicated and particularly long-term medical problems, not because of any failings of the staff but because there were just too many patients. There was not the laboratory back-up nor specialised diagnostic facilities needed, and there was no system of follow-up.

At the end of my time in the hospital, I was approached by a deeply unpleasant man who was clearly a member of the Mukhabarat (the Security Services). Though, of course, he got short shrift, it was not long after that my dear friend Leila started to cold-shoulder me in a very public and obvious way, following this up by saying to me with considerable embarrassment, "I think it would be better, in fact I have been told, that you should not continue sharing my office any more."

Later on, we found ourselves by chance alone in the basement getting coffee from the coffee machine. "It was too bad they made me say that," she said. "After all, you are my best friend in Baghdad."

For years I did not see her after this, nor did I have any news of her. I dared not write to her for fear it could endanger her in some way. It was only many years later I discovered she had left Iraq and was able to have the great pleasure of talking to her again.

On another occasion, I met a second very pleasant woman

doctor at an official ladies' gathering, who later on rang me up asking me and my husband to lunch. I feared she must be very naïve even to suggest such a thing, and that it would almost certainly put her and her husband in great danger. I felt compelled to say that we would love to come but I thought she ought to consult her friends first to make sure it would really be safe. If it was, she must ring back and there was nothing we would like more. I never heard another word.

One British man we knew did seem to have an easy and friendly relationship with the Mayor of Baghdad and was able to drop in and see him informally in the evening at his house as the occasion arose. But the end of the story was that the Briton was imprisoned in Abu Ghraib prison for eight years and the Mayor and his deputy (a woman) were hung. It was one of the saddest results of Saddam's regime that we were unable to meet Iraqis in anything but a strictly professional capacity. There were so many highly educated and westernised Iraqis, who in all their fields were at least the equal of the Europeans and many of whom would surely have become friends for life. No doubt it was fear of this that made the system so harsh, and so cleverly ensured that the very people who would most like to break the barrier, were forced, if they had any conscience, to be most careful not to.

At this time Iraq was engaged in a bitter war with Iran. Doctors at the hospital were at pains to point out to me that the Iranians were the aggressors and had been lobbing rockets and shells into Iraq before Saddam invaded, though the bellicose propaganda painting him as a follower of great Arab war heroes and a new caliph made that claim very unlikely. There was very little news of the progress of the fighting, which observers described as the war between the fat men and the thin men: the well-armed, overweight and reluctant Iraqis who liked their comforts and were almost outraged to find themselves sent to the front line, and the thin, virtually unarmed but fanatical Iranians who fought like tigers regardless of terrible casualties. Even so on the one occasion when I was able to discuss it with a girl soldier who was driving me to see an isolation hospital, I was told the Iraqi casualties were terrible and that every family she knew had lost at least one member. She cited one instance where three sons were fighting at the front. Their parents were amazed and alarmed when Saddam suddenly came to visit them. As they hastened to welcome him in a suitable manner, the garden gate opened and a coffin was carried in, followed by a second one and then a third. All three sons had been killed.

One of the spin-offs of the war was that food supplies were very scarce. The supermarkets seemed to sell only Turkish breakfast cereals (really just chaff) and whisky. I had never before seen anyone leave a supermarket with a trolley piled with twenty or thirty whisky bottles, let alone in a predominantly Islamic country. Foreigners were allowed to buy chickens when available at vast expense and inconvenience at a foreigners' shop, and at intervals were able to import supplies by air. All of the diplomatic ladies found themselves at once involved in a hunter-gatherer society at which some of them were very good. It was widely believed that the Americans and the French, who helped the regime with arms equipment and intelligence, got special treatment, whereas the UK was the bottom of the list because, contrary to popular belief, they did not do so. The real star was the German Ambassador's wife who spotted a lorry carrying potatoes and followed it like a blood- hound till it finally stopped and she managed to persuade them to sell her a sack. This was considered a notable triumph and filled the other diplomatic wives with equal feelings of envy and inadequacy.

It was not easy to produce traditional official meals, yet a lot of entertaining went on. Contrary to popular belief diplomatic entertaining is not about having a good time (though hopefully it is that too), but is about serious networking and can be very hard work. Curiously, the fact that it is often beset with formality and protocol usually makes it easier than a very informal approach because it provides a template that people of very different cultures can relate to and accept. I was interested in Baghdad to see it working at one party given just after a surprise move by the very secretive Iraqi government. No one knew what was behind this, but everyone had an opinion. As the evening wore on a consensus began to emerge as all these points of view were aired, and by the end of the evening a reasonable and acceptable explanation appeared to have been found.

Except for the French who had, as might have been expected, a highly trained highly paid chef imported from France. Good cooks were very difficult to find. The regime did everything possible to make it difficult for Embassy foreign workers to stay for long, presumably because if they did so they were likely to build up a relationship of loyalty towards their employers. We had hoped an excellent Jordanian cook who we knew and liked would join us in Baghdad, but when his family heard of his intention they were aghast and absolutely forbade him to do such a thing. After we had been there a while, we understood and agreed they had been right. If for some reason the regime had decided to take him into custody there would have been nothing we could have done to help or save him. So for a while I had to do the cooking for official parties of thirty or more, with the added complication that the food was so scarce and most of the ingredients had to be flown in from abroad. It is one thing to produce a big party for friends when if anything goes wrong you can laugh it off, and quite a different matter to produce a slap-up meal under the critical eyes of the serried ranks of foreign ambassadors' wives, particularly as there had been no time in my previous life to learn fancy cookery. What with the heat, the impossible kitchen and the endless official meals with no ingredients to cook, it could become very trying and I was always on tenterhooks till the meal was over. At last we found Rukhni, a small Bangladeshi cook, whose strong point was fish. He was very good at cooking fish and, if not engaged in that, could be found up to his knees in our small garden pond sorting out the goldfish. He was also interested in growing things and took a keen interest in the seedlings I was growing up for the garden. I thought my worries were at an end, but there were still problems. He was quite unable to forward-plan and, even though we had gone over together exactly what ingredients were needed for the menu for a party, he would still, three hours or less before the start of the meal, be out in the Souk trying to find something he had forgotten. At a less busy moment, on one occasion we were talking to him in our small upstairs galley kitchen and he was telling us about conditions in Bangladesh and what life was like there under the British.

"In those days," he said, "the poor people had justice. Now there is no justice and they all fight amongst themselves." Getting more and more excited about the iniquities of the present rulers, he seized the largest kitchen knife he could find, and waving it about wildly, cutting and thrusting, he advanced towards us to illustrate the point. For a moment in that very small space, we feared we might become a sad Foreign Office statistic, but fortunately diplomacy prevailed. It was interesting that over the years quite a lot of people said to us, "The trouble with our country is that we were not colonised by the British."

When we went home on our summer leave, Rukhni was in charge of the house. He looked after the goldfish so well that on our return they appeared to have doubled in numbers and were now literally feeding out of his hand. He had also done some watering, unlike Kamil, the gardener, who was meant to have come every day and in fact only turned up briefly once a week if that, and had managed to turn the garden into a jungle at the same time as letting a whole batch of precious plants die. When I spoke to Kamil about this, every sort of reason was produced:

"He had come constantly, the shade was too deep, the plants were in pots, were not in pots," and so on and so on, then finally, "Lady, it was very hot." I did so understand!

There was another side to Kamil. He asked me to look at his little daughter, who was ill. I found she had a progressive and fatal genetic condition, which would cause increasing physical and mental deterioration and distortion of her features. There was no cure and it was quite likely other children would be affected. It would have been very hard to sack him.

In the meantime, Rukhni was getting on so well with the Embassy driver, Qadr, which was such an unlikely alliance, and Qadr was looking so particularly cheerful we became a little worried. Qadr was a large thuggish Kurd, who was, fairly or unfairly, generally believed to be a villain, entirely out for himself, and we feared he might be trying to entice Rukhni into some nefarious scheme. It was typical of him that he got bored of waiting in a traffic queue in one lane of the two-lane highway one evening and suddenly swerved into the opposite oncoming lane and charged up it at full speed, knocking over bollards as he did so, because it might be quicker. When, very briefly, we had a Filipino girl working in our house, the situation had to be controlled by the threat of instant dismissal if there were any more complaints about his behaviour.

But he also had another side to his nature. Soon after we came, it was announced with a great fanfare that he was expecting twins. When about seven months later the heralded babies arrived and turned out to be two little girls, I greatly feared that this most macho of men would be disgusted and totally uninterested because they were not boys. Not a bit of it. He doted on them. Everyone had to admire them. I had to check them out medically to make sure all was well. And when a little later a trade fair came to Baghdad, all the participants, no matter what their speciality or country, were approached by this tough burly man and implored to sell him the one vital thing for his little girls' survival, which was talcum powder!

The most difficult thing to deal with in Iraq was the intense monitoring and control of diplomats throughout the country. As was to be expected, our two morning cleaners were obviously under the control of the Mukhabarat. The older one, an Assyrian Christian, had one morning off a week to enable her to report our doings to them. The other one, an Egyptian, was certain to be busy sweeping or dusting well within earshot, just behind the door, if ever I had a visitor, or hastily straightening out the papers on my husband's desk that she had been reading when I happened to come in. She had a hard life supporting a feckless husband and two little children in Egypt that she missed dreadfully, and presumably would not have had a job if she did not co-operate in this way. We assumed the house was bugged, and were amused when worldly-wise visitors would pause during a conversation, gesture towards the ceiling light, where they assumed the device would be, and then say slowly and carefully just what they wanted the Iraqis to hear.

It was interesting that colleagues who had served behind the Iron Curtain, including in Russia, told us this was by far the strictest regime they had encountered. It is extraordinarily difficult to be in a situation where you can never do what you want to do but only what you are allowed to do. We were not allowed to leave the town without official permission, which had to be applied for about a week before and might be granted or might not, often at the last moment, or even refused on the very morning of departure when all our arrangements had been made. If we were allowed to go and were, for instance, interested in seeing some archaeological site, it was to be expected there would be a white Mukhabarat Mercedes waiting for us when we arrived. On the one occasion we visited Kurdistan, we started with an escort of one car, to which was added another car containing three men, later joined by yet another vehicle with four armed soldiers, and finally a bus with at least 15 soldiers. We were in serious danger of developing a *folie de grandeur*.

In the town where we stayed, the hotel was patrolled all night. I could not decide whether all this was for our protection or to prevent my husband indulging in some nefarious plot with the Kurds, or perhaps a mixture of both. The effect of this was to produce a feeling of intense claustrophobia. It was a wonderful moment when we first left the city after our arrival and picnicked by a little river and heard the desert wind in the reeds, a symbol of the freedom we none of us had.

Occasionally I was allowed to mingle with Iraqi women at official women's gatherings. One of these was to celebrate Saddam's birthday. We all gathered in a large room and, after a certain amount of food and chat, there was a commotion at one of the doors and there entered two ladies carrying huge cathedral candles, followed by a large impressive lady with clasped hands, who suddenly flung her arms wide revealing the word SADDAM inscribed on her ample bosom. Behind were two more candle bearers and a lady carrying an enormous birthday cake. All the guests broke into cries of "Saddam, Saddam, Saddam", clapping and bouncing in their seats as they chanted, and then were served with slices of the cake. I couldn't help wondering what Saddam's wife, who was present, thought about this almost deification of her husband.

In fact, it was said many women were very impressed with Saddam, who had done great things for women's rights. One of the most obvious was the formation of women's choirs and groups, which appeared in public singing patriotic songs. The reason behind this was it abolished the traditional idea that women must not appear in public or voice their opinions in mixed gatherings. It emphasised the fact they were to have equal education with men and were not debarred from top responsible jobs. It was, for instance, common to see construction billboards, where public works were being undertaken, and read that the person in charge was a woman. A very important law had just been passed which, in cases of divorce, gave a mother equal rights with the father over custody of the children. Until that time, under Islamic law this right is given only to the father so that in practice, though the man could divorce his wife, his wife would never divorce him because it would mean losing her children.

But in spite of these undoubtedly beneficial reforms, the core of Saddam's Iraq was the Mukhabarat and their torture chambers. Some of the expatriates working there seemed able to ignore this and enjoy such social life and facilities as were available. But for many, and surely for all the Iraqis themselves, this was the black horror at the centre of their lives; not insulated in another country thousands of miles away, nor in another century hundreds of years ago, but here in this town, in the prison just over the horizon, going on every day, part of the work of the State, meticulously recorded and filed by an army of officials, just like any other civil service reports. However well a person did, however careful or discreet, at any time by some slip of the tongue or mistake, or malice or indiscretion of a friend, they could fall into the abyss – they and their families, even the smallest children. There was a moment in the hospital when some disappointed patient complained about some of the doctors. For several days, the fear and tension was everywhere until it was sorted out.

I met a British business man who described to me what one Iraqi had been brave enough to tell him:

"They hung me up by my thumbs, for four days and nights they hung me naked. They beat me all the time. I could hear the screams all round me. 'Tell us, tell us,' they said over and over again. I had nothing to tell. Nothing. In the end, I just talked. I said I met my friend in the coffee shop. I told them lies, lies. God forgive me, what could I do? You cannot imagine the pain. A lot of us did not survive. They said I was lucky. I wonder. They did much worse things, things you could not believe. They said if I told anyone, they would take me back. Even my wife doesn't know. I never talk to anyone now, I shouldn't have talked to you. I never stop thinking about it."

The cult of Saddam was all-pervasive. Wherever you went, he was portrayed in pictures, hoardings and statues in his many different roles. He was the wise statesman, the father of his people, the comforter of the sick, the friend of little children, the heroic warrior, the latter-day Caliph, almost like God. The only news in the newspapers were accounts of his doings, the TV reported only his speeches and activities. There were no foreign newspapers or magazines, no foreign news except the BBC World Service, if we could get it, and an international telephone service that very seldom worked. The effect of this over a period of many months was a growing feeling of isolation. More and more, the outside world became increasingly distant, like a mirage, as if this extraordinary claustrophobic country was the whole world and nothing else existed.

This was brought home to me by an incident that was started inevitably by the German Ambassador's wife, who said she had found oranges in the Souk. No one had seen oranges for months and I had an official dinner to arrange and no obvious food for it. I felt I had to go and see. The Souk, as expected, had nothing, but someone indicated I might find some by the river. I set off in that direction. It was winter and a grey Baghdad day – grey sky, grey earth, grey dusty trees, a grey haze over everything. Down by the river, a man in a little shop, after his first flicker of disquiet, told me he had none but there might be some "over there", pointing to a large walled garden across some waste land. I could see he wanted to be rid of me and didn't believe him, but it was just worth a try.

On the other side of the garden wall was a very unpromising door, which I felt sure would be locked, but I tried it all the same. I found myself in an orange grove full of large trees with shiny vivid green leaves, hung with enormous oranges, like glowing orange lamps. Under the trees and all around them were further mounds of brilliant fruit in great pools and splashes of colour. The earth was a rich warm brown colour, sprinkled with yellow leaves. At that very moment, the sun suddenly came out, cascading over everything till it shone and sparkled like quicksilver. An old man came towards me – an old, bent, weathered peasant with a wrinkled face and smiling eyes.

"Good morning, lady," he said, "You are welcome."

"You have oranges?" I said, hardly daring to believe my eyes. "Would you sell me some?"

"But of course. How many do you want?" I felt sure he would vanish into thin air in a minute but, throwing caution to the winds, I asked if I could have a box of them.

"It is my pleasure," he replied. "My son will weigh them."

Underneath the trees sat the whole family: the old grandmother, the two sons, the daughters-in-law, a host of small children laughing and playing. The women smiled their welcome and started talking to me while I waited for the fruit to be collected. They were not at all afraid; they were lovely, friendly, ordinary people. Suddenly, I was back in the real world again, where you could laugh and talk and love, where families were not suspicious of each other or of strangers, a world of colour where the sun shone. I could hardly believe it and, when the crate of oranges was carried up, found it very difficult to tear myself away.

The oranges were a great success and I got great kudos from having found them, but nobody knew how wonderful this discovery of the real world seemed. I was determined to go back but did not want to chance my luck, so I waited two weeks, hugging the secret to myself till I went again. I drove up to the wall, got out and saw two large planks had been nailed across it. "Forbidden to Enter" was written in big black letters across it. As I looked, a white alashni drew up near me. A young, smartly dressed man with a gold wristwatch and a revolver in a holster got out and shouted at me furiously, "Go away, go away. Forbidden. Forbidden."

I got back into my car, and drove back over the waste land, past the sentries with their walkie-talkies and the plastic bags and the grey trees and the pewter-coloured sky. There was not a real world after all.

Of course, it was not all gloom and doom. Iraq has some of the most fascinating and important archaeology in the world, it is after all the cradle of civilisation, and has wonderful sites to visit if it is allowed.

"How many miles to Babylon?"
"Three score miles and ten."
"Can I get there by candlelight?"
"Yes, and back again.
If your heels are nimble and light,
You can get there by candlelight."

Still, after thousands of years, Babylon holds a kind of magic in our imagination, this amazing city rising out of the mists of history. Sadly, the ruins of Babylon, which are close to Baghdad and easy to visit, have very little of that atmosphere. Too much has been destroyed, too little of the vast buildings and wonders of the early city remain. The massive Isshtar Gate, a huge double-arched structure preceded by a great processional way, has been taken to Berlin and re-erected there. The bricks are glazed in blue enamel and overlaid with pictures of animals and mythical beasts, and the approach road also lined with glazed brick walls is immensely impressive. But in Babylon itself there is only a small mock-up of part of this structure, which was erected by Saddam, in which he compares himself to Nebuchadnezzar. There are low remains of palaces and buildings but the Hanging Gardens and the great Walls, which were considered two of the Wonders of the Ancient World, are gone. You can see where the Tower of Babel stood, but nothing of it has been left standing. Only the Processional Way, which led from the Isshtar Gate into the heart of the city, gives a feeling of what it might have been like to enter this place for the first time and the impact it must have had, for instance, on foreign slaves as they were marched in and realised with despair there would be no hope of escape.

By the waters of Babylon we sat down and wept, when we remembered thee, oh Zion. As for our harps, we hung them up upon the trees that are therein. How can we sing the Lord's song in a strange land?

And looking out over the flat lands, one can understand the homesickness of the little Medean princess whose husband built her the Hanging Gardens to comfort her, when what she really wanted was a sight of the beloved mountains of her home.

The palaces of the Assyrians at Nineveh near Mosul have much more atmosphere. They are huge and dark with walls covered with reliefs of lion hunts and wars, rooms for audiences with the King and, to guard the entrances, statues of winged lions and two colossal winged bulls with human faces, which were there to protect the Ruler and were thought to know if anyone with subversive thoughts or plans was trying to see him. People waiting for an audience would be able to study at their leisure the horrors of Assyrian warfare and the fate that awaited any rebellious city, which are portrayed on the walls in gruesome detail. They would also have known of the sickening cruelties which King Assurbanipal describes in detail that he inflicted on his enemies. "After all," as someone wryly said, "he had an empire to govern!"

Yet this same King was also a notable scholar and had a large library of very important texts on such things as mathematics, astronomy and history, as well rituals and omens. And his father, Sennacherib, was noted for his interest in irrigation, agriculture and the planting of orchards and trees, and even had a nature reserve. Perhaps a famous contemporary picture sums up Assyrian culture best. King Assurbanipal is reclining on a couch in a tree-filled garden with his wife sitting beside him. They are drinking wine and retainers are bringing food. There is a man playing a harp and, to add the final touch, the head of the King's enemy hanging on a tree nearby.

In the soft earth of these plains, excavation reveals many layers of geological strata. There were clearly many floods of varying severity but one particular layer, said to be eight feet deep in some places, is regarded by some as evidence of the Great Flood. This is confirmed by a text called the Epic of Gilgamesh, written about 2200 BC, about this man who probably lived at least 500 years earlier. Gilgamesh was a Middle Eastern hero, who roamed the area doing what Middle Eastern heroes do. In his account, the chief god became irritated with men, not because they were wicked but because they made too much noise. He decided to drown them all to shut them up. However, another god felt this was a bit unfair and warned a very upright man called Utnapishtim of what was proposed. Utnapishtim followed the god's instructions and built a boatg in which he, his wife and sons and their precious seed, and the "game of the field" were able to survive. Gilgamesh was obsessed with finding the secret of eternal life and later went to visit Utnapishtim and hear his story, thinking he might know how to avoid death. In another account there is a description of what it was like when the waters finally went down: "And the whole earth was flat like the roof of a house."

Looking out over the plains, you suddenly realise that must have been exactly what it would have looked like, a uniform smooth flat covering of mud and sand as far as the eye could see – surely an extraordinarily vivid eye-witness account from 5000 years ago.

The archaeological museum in Baghdad was probably the most fascinating in the world. These wonderful artefacts –

statues, busts, wall engravings, golden treasure and priceless cuneiform texts – stretched back in time to the birth of civilisation. The most striking exhibits were from the Royal Graves of Ur: a beautiful and intricate golden woman's headdress, a large lyre ornamented with a golden bull's head, a golden ram caught in a thicket, and numerous gold and lapis lazuli ornaments and other jewels. Even more sensational was the story behind these treasures. Ur was an important city in the south of the country built by the Sumerians, the oldest culture in the region in 2600 BC. There is still standing there a huge ziggurat, or stepped pyramid of vast proportions, now partially restored, which was central to their rituals and worship, and the scene of religious processions when the priests ascended to the top of the building, symbolising their approach to the heavens and to God. Some have suggested the story of Jacob's dream of angels ascending and descending from heaven was an echo of these events, and his grandfather Abraham was, of course, reported to have been born in the city.

Leonard Woolley excavated a series of 16 graves here, some of which were of a King and a Queen. In the case of the Queen, she was found with her beautiful padded headdress of intricate gold and lapis lazuli on her head, and another one beside it, and two crouching female figures next to her. Just adjoining this chamber was another grave containing 74 bodies, of whom 68 were female. They were lying on their sides in neat rows, the heads of the inner rows resting on the feet of the preceding row. All wore elaborate gold bejewelled headdresses and ornaments, bright red jackets, and had their hair tied with gold or silver ribbons, except for one, whose ribbon was still in her pocket. "As if," said Woolley, "she had been late for her own funeral."

There was no sign of violence or distress, and each of them had a goblet in her hand, and there was a large cauldron on one side. Woolley's interpretation of these findings (though they are not now accepted by everyone) was that they were willing victims, believing they were accompanying their royal master and mistress to a more glamorous afterlife, and that they died peacefully having drunk poison from the cauldron.

One of the many tragedies of the misguided invasion of Iraq is that the Americans allowed the museum to be looted, and many of these priceless treasures have been lost.

There was one other visit in Iraq which stands out in my mind and that was to the Shia Shrine at Kerbala. The Iraqi Women's Federation issued an invitation to the diplomatic wives to be shown this shrine, which is one of the holiest Shia places, built over the tomb of the Prophet's grandson Hussein, who was killed here in 680 AD and became the third Imam. We gathered together in front of the entrance and were briefed on what to do.

"Now, ladies, you must cover yourselves completely apart from your faces, and be particularly careful not to show any hair." We struggled to obey, finding our slippery abbayas surprisingly difficult to manage, particularly when it came to keeping them low down on our foreheads. When she was finally satisfied with our appearance and with our faces further concealed by sunglasses, she turned and led us through the gates. That we, foreigners, infidels, and women at that, were allowed in was amazing.

As we passed through the shadow of the gateway into the sunlight beyond, we entered another world. The great paved court spread out around us, with its high mediaeval walls shutting out the dust and noise of the town surrounding it. In the centre the Shrine itself, a rectangular building the size of a small church, rose to a glittering golden dome, round which pigeons circled in an intensely blue sky. The colour of the sky was repeated in the patterned blue tiles covering all the walls, interspersed here and there with blue-green and brown, blending into a varied and wonderfully harmonious whole.

The court was full of people but not crowded: they walked to and fro or sat talking in low voices. There were merchants from the Souk outside, an old granny with her little grandson astride her shoulders, the soldier just back from the Front, the taxi driver, the young girls, and the housewife carrying her shopping, the youths, the mullahs, and the Hajis with their white turbans who had made the pilgrimage to Mecca. It was a microcosm of the city.

When we reached the Shrine itself, we left our shoes at the kiosk at the gate and walked barefoot to the main entrance, passing little family groups or single people, sitting quietly reading or praying. Then there were more shadows as we passed through the door and were in the interior itself. It was breathtaking. All of the upper walls and ceiling were made of cut glass, sparkling in the light of hundreds of chandeliers. It was like walking into a brilliantly lit diamond. If a Gothic cathedral portrays in stone the concept of worship, then this Shrine is the expression of glory, the blazing unbelievable glory of God, shouting and reverberating from a thousand points of light. A message conveyed without any need of words.

Of course, there were some things that seemed strange to Western eyes. The men and women pray in separate parts of the building but, in a Muslim country, any other arrangement would be too distracting. Whilst we were there, a group of chanting men carrying a shrouded corpse on a bier entered, circled the central tomb three times, and then left. Later we were taken to a kind of side chapel and much was made of the red-veined marble on the walls, representing the blood of Hussein, who was killed on that very spot. Many people condemn the Shias as followers of a perverted necrophilic religion obsessed with blood and death. But the Shias recoil with horror at the Christian portrayal of the crucified Christ and tortured saints. And when we deplore the fanatical frenzy of some of the Shia crowds we see on television, we should remember there were times when Christians behaved with similar or worse fanaticism, and try to remember the beauty and sanctity of a place like Kerbala.

Since the invasion of Iraq, thousands of Iraqis have fled their country. Dr. Rahim, now a refugee in England, has told me that, in spite of the dreadful cruelties of Saddam, if you kept your head down and were very careful, it was possible to live a more or less normal life, but that now this is out of the question and it is so dangerous, particularly if you are educated, that he and his family had been forced to leave the country. I remember my talk with the consultant in the hospital: "If we get rid of him, we will get someone worse, believe you me, we will."

BALTISTAN

In 1981 my husband and I decided to visit our eldest son, now grown up, who was working for the ODA in Pakistan. We joined up with a niece and her husband, a New Zealander who was also a diplomat with professional duties in the area. Having all met in Islamabad, we planned to fly to Skardu, the capital of Baltistan, which is a remote area of Kashmir, and to travel from there by road up the Indus Gorge to Gilgit and Hunza, after spending a few days in Skardu.

We flew up to Skardu in a little Fokker plane. It was a spectacular flight, as we rose over the foothills north of Islamabad and the mountains gradually marched towards us; at first distant, then closer and closer, the great climbers' peaks, Rakaposhi, K2, and on our right, Nanga Parbat. Its huge bulk towered above our right wing, shouldering up through precipices of ice thousands of feet high, the graveyard of at least 80 climbers who still lie unburied on its frozen sides. Then we cleared a neck of the mountains, skimmed over an upland plateau and dived into a gorge so narrow that, as we twisted and turned down it, our wing tips seemed nearly to touch the sides. The undercarriage came down for landing with nothing but rock walls around us. What a relief when suddenly we emerged over the plain of Skardu and saw the runway beneath us!

The plain of Skardu has that luminous sun-bleached quality that one associates with very high mountains. It is flat, with the Indus flowing gently towards its Gorge between banks of pale yellow sand, and the mountains of the Karakoram, with their white peaks, a blue encircling wall. The poplar trees stood in palisades of white trunks, their leaves beginning to yellow in the autumn sun, and on the alluvial fans at the side, the fields at their feet were a shimmer of green.

"It never rains in Baltistan," they told us; but by the morning of the third day it had done just that for the past twelve hours. However, there was no suggestion that this might in any way hinder our journey and we set off early in great spirits, expecting to be in Gilgit by teatime. We were soon running along the road on the side of the Gorge. The mountains here fall to the river in one sheer sweep, almost perpendicular, dark brown walls of mud and rock thousands of feet high, turning black in the rain, with outcrops of enormous cliffs from which boulders the size of houses have fallen. If the clouds cleared for a moment above the black walls, we could see the snowcovered Karakorum Range, rising peak after peak above them. In some places the valley widens sufficiently for a few terraced fields and perhaps a cluster of huts. Mostly it narrows, totally barren, without grass, flowers, or any living thing. The road twists along the side, cut into the slope or under rock

112

overhangs, and far below the grey waters of the Indus foam and roar over the rapids. This is not userfriendly country, though quite how unfriendly we did not realise as we set out.

We came across a slide, most of which had already been cleared away, and increasing numbers of boulders strewn on the road which had to be negotiated. A falling stone hit us but was nothing to worry about. We stopped for tea at a little tea-house proudly called the Chanandar Hotel. It was a miserable leaking wooden hut. The owner, wrapped in his brown shawl, was sitting on top of the oven, in which a fire burned. It was warm in there and the tea was milky and very sweet. We looked through a doorway into the main room beyond.

"Good Lord!" we said laughing. "Fancy having to spend a night in there!", little knowing that in three days' time it would seem like a palace.

As we drove on, the landslides became more frequent. On one or two occasions they were quite difficult to negotiate and it was better not to look too closely at the precipice on the outer side. Eventually we arrived at a very large mud slip covering the road between two cliffs. Several vehicles were already there waiting to get through, and a Pathan Commando Colonel in camouflage battle dress with a maroon beret stuck at a jaunty angle on his head appeared to be directing operations. He had just fallen down in the mud but emerged roaring with laughter. A group of men started to move the large boulders that had been swept down with the mud, the passengers picked their way across and, one by one, the vehicles followed until it came to the turn of a large lorry, which gave up in the middle, completely stuck .The way back was now blocked, but the Colonel, who was travelling to Gilgit with his Adjutant, was certain we would get through that night. It was becoming quite an adventure and all the more enjoyable for that, though when we set off again, we were pleased we now had a competent guide and were with other travellers.

The rain increased, the rocks and slides on the road grew more frequent. Then, as night was falling, we reached the moment of truth about our journey, when we turned a corner and saw two impassable landslides blocking the road ahead of us. The half dozen or so jeeps and other assorted vehicles which had met up by chance on the road and now formed an informal convoy were parked as close as they dared to the outer precipice, and as far as possible away from a wicked-looking black cliff towering above us. We had just manoeuvred them with the greatest difficulty through a narrow gully below this cliff, which had been almost blocked by a series of enormous boulders that had fallen from the rock face. Now, as we contemplated the obstacles ahead, the only option seemed to be to try to return the way we had come. As we waited, there was a sound of falling rocks pouring down the mountainside, all the more unnerving because it was impossible to see them coming. They cascaded over the cliff 20 yards behind us and settled in the road in a cloud of dust. In the gully the leading jeep was through, but the next one got stuck, and a large boulder crashing down from the cliff seriously damaged its side. Suddenly we realised we had to get out of there fast. In a very short time we had packed our rucksacks with what we might need for the night and the last person had left the gully at a run as two further rock slides tumbled across the road. We were 90 kilometres from base, in pouring rain, without shelter, on the side of a mountain, which we now realised was completely rotten. Even the apparent safety of overhangs was illusory when we saw the jagged rocks that fell from their roofs. And night was falling.

We trudged back along the road in the relentless rain and in about five kilometres came to another chai khana, or tea house, we had passed on the way. Beyond the outer room with its cooking stove was a large room already full of travellers in woolly hats and shawls. The roof made of poplar logs was leaking, the floor was awash and the stove round which a crowd of people were huddling was smoking furiously, only a little of the smoke escaping through a hole in the roof. We managed to annex two of the string beds arranged round the room, and three filthy quilts, then as darkness fell, prepared as best we might to spend the night; at least it was better than the bare mountainside.

It was dark by six and at seven two little boys appeared with a Primus and started to cook rice. It took them hours and, when it was finished, they served everyone else in the room but us. Only at the insistence of a friendly Pathan who spoke English did they finally agree to give us any. The rain was no, if anything, heavier than before, and a necessary trip outside, with the ground a lake and the sound of falling landslides all around, was a very discouraging affair. By nine o'clock, with only a flicker of light from a lantern, everyone in the room, with a lot of hawking and spitting, was settling down to sleep. Five large people on two small beds, made of string and steel rods and wire specially designed to stick into whoever uses them, is not a recipe for a good night. I dozed off and woke in the dark, thankfully convinced it must be at least three in the morning. It was only eleven! There was no sleep after that. A drip from the roof crept up the bed from our feet. The fire smoked. People spat and talked and snored. A lantern flared and lit dimly seen figures wrapped in shawls and then died down again. Outside the mountain continued to fall about us. It was a very long night.

At six o'clock the next morning, when it became light, the little boys returned. Everyone in the room was given tea except us, who they refused to serve. We realised it was going to take many days to unblock the road and, apart from packets of biscuits, there was no reliable source of food. Another night in the chai khana was unthinkable. It was agreed the two youngest men should walk to a police post three kilometres further back along the road. Here they found the Colonel installed.

"What do you advise?" they asked him. "We are a party of five. Two of us are women and two are over sixty. Shall we stay in the tea house or come up here?"

As they had hoped, he suggested we should join him, but warned there was no bedding or beds. After a furious argument with the proprietor of the chai khana, we persuaded him to loan us three even filthier and wetter quilts and, laden with them, we walked up to the police post, strung out along the rockstrewn road, so that if anyone was buried by a landslide, there would be someone to dig him or her out.

Pakistanis like family parties, and we were received with great kindness by the Colonel and his Adjutant. The Colonel was an impressive tough man of about forty, and his Adjutant a cheerful brigand with a wicked sense of humour.

"You will be fed," they said – a very welcome promise for we felt sure that, if any food was going, the Colonel Sahib would get hold of it. He had already collected around himself a motley group of benighted travellers. There were three botanists, two of them Japanese; an elderly Pakistani merchant banker and his wife and niece; a honey moon couple; an English banker; a jolly plump man who carried all his worldly goods tied up in a tablecloth on his head; and an old man in a shawl whose wise lined face earned him the name of the Philosopher. In the cheerful atmosphere of the Colonel's mess, amid a lot of friendly banter, this strangely assorted group was quickly to become a close-knit band of brothers. Because I was the mother of our son and had grey hair, I was treated with particular kindness. I became "Mum" to all the rest of the party, was given the first helping at meals and the most comfortable seat and, most welcome of all in the days to come, would have my pack carried for me.

That afternoon, encouraged by a meal of hot rice and tea, the three men walked back to the stranded vehicles and brought out all our remaining luggage. It was an enormous relief when they returned, exhausted and soaking but safe; the crumbling mountains were far too dangerous for comfort. We lay that night on our damp quilts on the concrete floor of the small police cell that had been allotted to us, side by side like sardines in a tin, and laughed and laughed at the absurdity of the situation, and with relief that we were no longer in the Terrible Tea House.

The next morning the Colonel had news. The road was blocked for the next 50 kilometres, but we would walk out to an Army Post 16 kilometres away starting "Now". All our belongings were quickly stuffed into rucksacks, leaving our suitcases behind, and off we went. The old man of 72, with his wife in her sari and slippers, who had never walked farther than her kitchen in years, were the biggest worry but, dogged and uncomplaining, they plodded along at the rear, with the Colonel, the epitome of macho masculinity, without the slightest sign of impatience and with the greatest courtesy, strolling beside them like a sheepdog rounding up his flock.

We had a brief ride on a tractor between landslides but it did not last long. At the end of it there was talk of a payment of 400 rupees, but the Philosopher soon put a stop to that and the driver left happily with 20. Then there was more walking and finally the Chanandar Hotel came in sight. What luxury! Dry, not too dirty, with hot chapattis and tea – how could we ever have despised it? Suddenly, out of nowhere, an army truck appeared and we were whirled up the last few miles to the Army Post and the Civil Hospital, where we were to spend the night.

Here indeed was a five-star hotel. A ward that was clean, dry and definitely warm, three beds for five people, two blankets to a bed, even an inside loo. The doctor in charge said the place was besieged by people wanting shelter, the unprecedented rain was a natural disaster and the local houses were quite unable to stand up to it. That night, for the first time, the three Pakistani ladies were allowed to join everyone else at supper. Sitting on the floor amongst the younger men, the two girls soon made up for lost time. Elderly auntie lying exhausted on the sofa was clearly worried at such unorthodox behaviour, but fortunately she was so tired she fell asleep and did not spoil the fun.

We were ready to start at 7.30 the next morning. The Colonel's men we heard had driven from Skardu as far as they could to a landslide 30 kilometres along the road. A party had set out from there at five that morning and were even now walking in to meet us. Everyone was a little tense, there were 20 kilometres to cover and we must start at once if we wanted to be out by nightfall. We had a short ride in a truck, a pause for some engineers to blow up four enormous boulders blocking the road, then reached a tremendous rock fall in an overhang barring our way. As we started climbing over it, there was a sudden shout and there were the Colonel's commandos, grinning from ear to ear, with enormous packs, advancing to meet us. Great was the rejoicing. As well as every kind of lethal weapon and sleeping bags, they carried Thermoses of hot tea and produced a meal of chapattis and omelettes. Away from the danger of the overhang, we settled down to this miraculous breakfast, with the Colonel surrounded by his men like a lion with his cubs.

Then we started to walk in earnest. We passed two hamlets. The people looked ill and drawn. They were not hostile but not friendly either, standing silent and staring. Many of them had thin torn clothes, and some of the elderly crept by with enormous loads in baskets on their backs. The women veiled their faces and took quick fascinated glances at us without appearing to. They all looked undernourished and desperately poor.

The hours passed. The party became strung out along the road, everyone at the Colonel's suggestion going at his or her own pace. We paused briefly to eat our last remaining biscuits, then went on again. Some of the Commandos thought they might find a jeep in a village on the other side of the Gorge, but we did not want to wait. There were nine kilometres still to go and it was late afternoon. The sense of urgency we had felt all day increased. It would be dangerous in this place and this weather to be caught in the open as night fell. We went on walking . . . and walking, the road unwinding before us, the mountains black and menacing on either side. Even the youngest and toughest man in the party, carrying a very heavy load, began to tire. It got later still. Rounding a corner, we saw a tractor standing by a hut and paused to ask if there was a driver.

"No driver. Gone to Skardu."

"Is there a jeep?"

"No jeep."

"Oh dear, no jeep."

At that very moment came a noise on the road behind, getting louder and louder. Round the bend, with shouts, swept a vehicle pulling a trailer on which were piled all the rest of the party, with the Colonel cross-legged on a grid at the back, holding a Kalashnikov on his knee. There was just room for three of us, so the two younger men waited to be picked up next time. And we went off at breakneck speed, tearing round the bends on the twisting road. This was no time for Muslim etiquette, it was a case of seizing the nearest man and holding on for dear life. After clearing away two small landslides, we came to a final halt. Several landslides away, we saw in the distance an open road and two army trucks. It was dusk as we climbed over the last and biggest gash in the mountainside and walked towards our rescuers. But it was a long hour later, raining again in earnest and quite dark, before the last of the party were ferried to safety. We watched anxiously as they came towards us, helped over that treacherous terrain by the Commando's torches, our two men the last of all to arrive.

"But, Mum, you shouldn't have worried," said the Colonel. "You knew they would be all right if I was looking after them."

Thirty kilometres later, we were back at the Rest House we had left four days before. They had almost closed for the winter, but managed to find dry beds, food and even hot water in a jug. We gave the Colonel tea and the Adjutant whisky, and listened to him talk about the horrors of the Afghan War, his outrage and anger all the more moving for the restraint with which he spoke.

And then we were home. Our house seemed shamefully comfortable and cluttered. We often thought of those pinched faces and the torn clothes and leaking huts along the road, and of our chivalrous rescuers and our extraordinary luck in meeting up with them. As we fell asleep, we still marvelled at comfortable, warm, dry beds. And often we dreamt. It was not a nightmare, but there was a sense of urgency: there was a long way to go and we had to get out by nightfall.

PALESTINE

The first time we went to Lebanon, on our way to Qatar in 1959, we were walking along a mountain path when a party of women wearing long black robes heavily embroidered in scarlet thread, and white hijabis, scrambled up onto the path ahead of us.

"Who are they?" I asked my husband.

"Palestinian women from the refugee camp below," he replied.

At that time I was completely unaware of the Israeli/Palestine problem. As far as I was concerned, there was the Holy Land, which was Israel and was inhabited by Jews, as we had always been taught in the Bible. The fact that it had not been a Jewish state for 2000 years and, during that time, had been lived in by a different Arab race had never crossed my horizon. We left Lebanon for the Persian Gulf and, for the first time, I met Palestinians, not the simple peasants of popular perception but highly educated, articulate men and women, many of whom had become friends of my husband on previous visits to the Middle East. I became aware of the tragedy and burning sense of injustice they felt about expulsion from their native land, though some of them, amazingly, were prepared to consider some accommodation with the Israelis if these injustices were rectified. We used to go and visit schools where the teachers invariably put up maps of Palestine showing what had happened to their country, and were mostly vehemently anti-British because of Suez and the Israeli invasion of Palestine, for which they felt the Balfour Declaration was responsible.

Difficult though this situation was, one was forced to question whether the Israelis really had a right to this country they had left two millennia ago. Of course the Jews had a desperate need for security after the horrors of the Holocaust, but why should it be at the expense of a Middle Eastern race who had no responsibility at all for their treatment and in fact had always had very cordial relations with the Jews living in their midst?

It was at this point I first briefly visited Palestine. The Israeli presence was not very obtrusive then, though we did see parties of settlers, armed with guns, swaggering up the streets of Jerusalem in a very provocative way. The highlight of the visit for me was to be taken by a Palestinian friend to Bethlehem, where his family had a house. It was market day and the town was crowded. Everyone we saw was in traditional dress, the women particularly striking in their embroidered dresses and white head coverings. It was just like the pictures I had been brought up on as a child. I could imagine I was back in Biblical times and could easily believe the centuries-old tradition that the manger in the cave below the church was indeed the place where Christ was laid by his mother. To add to this Biblical atmosphere, we were taken to our friend's house just below the town in the Shepherds' Fields, where his wife had given birth a few days before to a little boy. She beckoned me over to her and whispered, "You know we say that if a woman is in labour and she prays for a friend that she too will become pregnant, it will come true. I prayed for you whilst I was having my son."

I have no doubt she did indeed do so, and was immensely touched that she should think of a foreign woman she did not know very well and with whom she had never discussed such a thing, during the overwhelming experience of giving birth. It was the sort of wonderfully warm-hearted gesture that Palestinians make when you least expect it, which melts your heart. Incidentally our first son was born about nine months later.

A little later, I became involved in a charity providing Medical Aid to the Palestinians and visited the country many times over the years starting in the 1960s. The first visit was a revelation. We drove to Hebron.

"We must look out for settlers," said the colleague who was driving us. "They may

shoot us if they see us."

There were many uprooted and cut-down olives lying by the road. It was explained to me that the Israelis did this so they could claim the land was not being farmed and it could be taken over by the state and given to settlers. When we reached the centre of the town, the place was in turmoil. A Jewish group had just taken over buildings in the centre of the market and intended to live there. They do so to this day, approximately 400 settlers amongst about 1,600 Arabs, with the life of the town entirely controlled for their benefit by Israeli soldiers sent to guard them. It was from this group that Baruch Goldstein came, who later entered the Mosque during Friday prayers and shot and killed 29 worshippers and wounded many more. He is revered by the settlers as a great hero.

Further afield, we drove through a pine forest recently set aside and planted by the Israelis, helped by generous donations from charities in Canada. It was wonderful to see these acres of beautiful trees, so much needed in this arid land. What was never revealed was that it necessitated the destruction of an entire Palestinian village in the centre of the area, the villagers, mostly women and children, being forced out of their homes without notice under the blazing July sun, without water or food, and all their houses demolished. The Canadian donors were apparently quite unaware that this had happened.

Later, in the north of the country we passed areas of farm land, where the Palestinian farmers were suffering serious problems of water shortage because they were only allowed to dig surface wells whilst the neighbouring settlers were allowed to sink artesian wells that reached underground aquifers and drained the surface water from their lands. Later still, in Gaza I met several farmers and always asked them how much land they farmed. They invariably replied, "At the moment I farm such and such a number of dunums."

"Why do you say 'at the moment'?" I asked.

"Because at any moment the Israelis can come and take more land from me."

In 1975, when we went to Jordan, we found that about 60 % of the population were Palestinian, refugees who had fled Palestine after the Israeli invasions, particularly in 1967. King Hussein had granted them Jordanian citizenship, and some had become successful entrepreneurs and professionals and built themselves large and impressive villas. Many of these people did not want to leave their houses in Amman but wanted to have a country they belonged to and could visit as they wished. But there still remained a large number of refugees in camps, no longer tented but more like small villages with little infrastructure.

To the north, further from Amman, in the forests of Ajlun, a lovely place of oaks and arbutus trees and a very good area for walks and picnics, were many deserted trenches and the debris of Palestinian fighters left behind by those who settled there after the defeat of 1967. It was a melancholy sight, a symbol of defeat and lost hopes and lives, and of a disastrous policy they pursued trying to establish a mini-state here from which to launch attacks on Israel. As the power of their position increased, they began to threaten King Hussein's authority,, and finally his life, by attacking a convoy in which he was travelling. The situation had become impossible and the King finally threw them out after bitter fighting and many casualties. Most of them then fled to Lebanon, where they again repeated the mistake of trying to set up another mini-state, and this was at least partially responsible for the outbreak of the Lebanese Civil War. Eventually all the fighters were expelled to Tunis, leaving their families behind in Lebanon. Immediately after the men left these 2000 defenceless women and children in Sabra and Shatila, the refugee camps were massacred by Ariel Sharon's Lebanese proxies.

When we went into the Jordanian countryside, it was quite usual to find in some remote place a young man or boy sitting under a tree, studying. Almost always they were Palestinians desperate to get an education. The medical charity that I was involved with had, amongst other things, focussed on the education of medical personnel in the Occupied Territories, with the aim of producing a core of people with first-class expertise, which would become the seed corn of a future Palestinian medical service. Many of the people we were involved with were experienced and knowledgeable, but hampered in the way they dealt with medical problems by their legacy of rote learning, with little critical analysis or questioning of supposed authority, which I would notice later in some of the students in Iraq. With it, in some cases, went a lack of the concept of Tender Loving Care, which was just as important and should be the basis of all medical practice. We were responsible for starting and training the first Intensive Care Unit in Gaza, and sent the newly formed team to finish their education in Addenbrooke's Hospital in Cambridge. They returned, saying, "Now we understand what you were trying to teach us."

They became very expert in their field and were able to pass on their skills by training others, as we had hoped. We discovered the Occupied Territories were full of store rooms of very expensive equipment donated by foreign charities lying unused, either because they had broken down and there was no one to mend them, or because no one had been trained in their use. As the years passed, so many of these gifts were destroyed or rendered useless in the episodes of violence and destruction engulfing the territory, but the well-trained people, unless they were killed, could continue to function and their training continue to be beneficial to the community. This kind of work continues to this day.

With their passion for education, one of the most difficult problems the Palestinians have to contend with is the obstacles that are put in their way in obtaining it. Such things as permits to attend a University for a degree course very often will not be granted or will not be for the required length of time, so that they cannot take their finals unless they overstay the time they are allowed to be there and are thereby liable to arrest. Children attending school are frequently harassed by settlers, and the continuous 24-hour curfews which have been imposed in some towns for days, weeks or, in one case, five months, in which the entire population is confined to their houses.

As the years passed, the Matrix of Control over the inhabitants of the Occupied Land became more and more severe and, in 2005, not having visited Palestine for some time, I joined a tour to plant olive trees in the area.

The olive tree planting movement is based on a desire to help the olive oil industry and promote Fair Trade. Thousands and thousands of these trees – the staple crop of the

Palestinians of the West Bank – have been, and continue to be, cut down by the Israelis. But a morning spent planting a few olives is not going to restore the farmers' livelihood. It is just part of an annual communal gesture to assert the Palestinians' right to their ancestral lands, and their determination not to be forced off them.

But another reason for going was a growing concern over very disturbing reports by Amnesty International and other agencies of the way medical emergencies were being treated at Israeli checkpoints in the Occupied Territories.

The verbatim account given by Maysoul from a village near Nablus was one of many.

Maysoul Saleh lives ten miles from Nablus, where she intended to deliver her first baby. When she went into labour, she was driven by her husband and father-in-law to the Howra checkpoint and ordered out of the car to produce their papers.

"We told the soldiers I had to go to hospital to give birth as soon as possible, that I was in severe pain. They first refused, then told me to uncover my belly, so they could see I was telling the truth. All this lasted about an hour and we were told to go ahead. We drove on and after a few hundreds of metres I heard shots from the front of the car. The car stopped and I saw that my husband had been shot in the throat and upper body, and was bleeding heavily. Soldiers came and pulled me out of the car. They made me take off all my clothes to examine me. Then they left me on the ground, bleeding from the wounds, and in labour. I asked for something to cover myself with, but they didn't give me anything. To this day I feel shame and anger about this." Her husband was by now dead. She gave birth to her child in a hospital lift.

Rula was told when she went into labour and had to go to the hospital, to go to a checkpoint, where the ambulance would meet her because it could not get past the road block.

She said, "We took a taxi because cars are not allowed near the checkpoint, and we walked the rest of the way. I was in pain. At the checkpoint there were several soldiers: they were drinking coffee and ignored us. My husband spoke to them in Hebrew; I was in pain and felt I was going to give birth there and then; I told my husband who translated what I said to the soldiers but they did not let us pass. I was lying on the ground and I crawled behind a concrete block by the checkpoint to have some privacy and gave birth there in the dust like an animal. I held the baby in my arms and she moved a little but after a few minutes she died in my arms." Her weeping husband cut the umbilical cord with a stone.

These are not isolated incidents. At least 55 women have been forced to deliver their babies at checkpoints and at least 23 of the babies have died. Other Palestinians with different dangerous conditions have been refused passage and perished. In view of this and so much more, how could one just pass by on the other side and not try to discover what was happening.

We started our tour in the Negev, the large triangular piece of land in the south of Israel. This arid area has traditionally been the home of the Palestinian Bedu. They are only semi-nomadic and spend at least part of the year growing crops, mainly wheat, on these ancestral lands. The Israelis have been pushing them into ever smaller and smaller areas until most of them have been forced to leave, or have been relocated in small towns with the minimum of infrastructure, no employment and, as a result, the total disintegration of their way of life and their society. At least 3000 of them are now refugees in Jordan or are forced to live in dreadful circumstances far away from their lands. One of these tribes, which I happened to know from previous visits with the medical charity, had been put in a barren valley just next door to the largest of Jerusalem's rubbish dumps. Two Israeli settlements on the hills on either side of the valley look down on them and one of these controls all their water. They are housed in steel containers used in shipping freight, totally uninsulated from the searing summer heat and the bitter winter cold, and when they built a school for their children, the settlers came down and destroyed it when the children were there.

Down in the Negev we met the head of one of these communities, a wiry tough little man who had been fighting a desperate legal battle for at least two years to prevent his tribe losing their lands. We saw large fields of spring wheat growing well and healthily but, in the middle, one very big area where the crops were very sparse, stunted and unhealthy. This was his land. The Israelis either ploughed up his crops as soon as they were planted, or harrowed them if they were a little bigger, or sprayed them with chemicals if they were bigger still, or with other poisons to make them inedible if they were about to be harvested. In this way he was left with no income and large debts for the seed corn and fertilisers he had to buy.

"All I want," he said with tears in his eyes, "is to bring up my son here and farm this land with him. This is such a beautiful place with this wonderful blue sky and the sun and the birds singing. If the Israelis just killed us, at least we would not feel any more."

A day or two later, we were staying with a Palestinian family in one of the farming villages in central Palestine, which is the centre of the olive-growing area. It is overshadowed by a steep hill, on the top of which, like a menacing predator, stands the huge settlement of Ariel, a town of 30,000 or 40,000 inhabitants. This is a very important area of the West Bank as one of the biggest aquifers is here, a vital resource in this dry land. The settlers take at least 80 % of the water, and spew their waste and sewage down the hill onto the villages below. Again, the Arabs, unlike the Israelis, are forbidden to sink deep artesian wells and do not have enough water to irrigate their crops, sometimes not even enough to drink.

Our host had been running an important charity, sponsored by the Australians, teaching improved techniques of dry-land farming, such as terracing, soil improvement and, most importantly, the breeding of drought-resistant crops. He had a lot of greenhouses, plants, seeds and a well-equipped office with files, computers, records, etc. One night the heavily armed settlers came down from the hill above and trashed everything – the plants, the precious seeds, the greenhouses, and everything in the office, which is now a ruined shell. A little later they returned again at night and forced him and his family, which included several small children, out of the house at gunpoint, seemingly just to harass them. There is, of course, no compensation, nor any suggestion of legal redress, and the charity has closed.

Further down the valley, the largest industrial development in this part of the Middle East has been erected by the Israelis on Arab land. It is considered too polluting to be built in Israel itself and has been cleverly sited so that the prevailing wind will blow the toxic fumes over the Palestinians, and the poisonous effluents can spill onto their land, where we could see they destroy the surrounding vegetation.

A farmer we met by chance on our travels down the valley, who, with typical Middle Eastern hospitality, immediately asked us into his house for coffee, told us how he felt about the occupation.

"The Israelis are like a man who takes my house and my land from me. I stand outside my house and he from inside the house asks me what I want and tells me to go away. And I say, 'All I want are my two peach trees so that I can look after them. You have taken everything, I just want my two trees.'"

Near the end of our visit we returned to Jerusalem. That evening we sat down for supper on the roof of an open-air restaurant in the Old City. It was a lovely warm evening, all around were the lights of the city, and in the distance the sound of chanting from some of the many churches. Across the table from me, we were joined by an American paediatrician, who had been working in the northern town of Jenin. Whilst he was there, he was walking with a colleague down a street, both of them in clothes which clearly proclaimed they were doctors. A tank appeared and one of the soldiers shot him in the face at point-blank range. By a miracle, neither his brain nor his spinal cord were injured but he was blinded in one eye and one side of his face was shattered. Now, after nine operations he had a recognisable face again, but it was clearly a sad travesty of what had once been that of a good-looking man.

The actual planting of olive trees took place in two fields on the last day of our tour. We joined the olive planters at a site in the Bethlehem area. Among the crowds of schoolchildren and their teachers, students, aid workers and well-wishers, geriatric grandmothers were not too common, so I soon found myself slipping into the classical Middle Eastern role of Ustaaz, or Professor, who stands about looking knowledgeable, holding the olive saplings and giving good advice, whilst all the hard work is done by a lad with a pickaxe. When the planting was completed, we climbed a steep hill out of the wadi to reach the transport that was to take us on. The hillside was scattered with clumps of brilliant scarlet anemones, the "lilies of the field" so vividly described in the gospels, still so beautiful and still flourishing amidst all the despair and suffering around us.

Great sweeps of settler roads divide up the country, with many new ones being built. They are large double carriageways, which Palestinians are not allowed to use or even to cross, and as most of the roads divide farmers from their fields. This means the crops cannot be tended, or perhaps only after lengthy journeys on poorly maintained side roads. All around us, Israeli settlements stood on every hill, the huge banks of white-walled houses like hostile battleships floating in a sea of olive trees, overlooking and controlling the Arab land and villages below. Bethlehem itself is no longer the bustling town I knew, with its market and crowds of tourists. There are many fewer visitors, and the city is entirely surrounded by the Wall, with only one access gate guarded by Israeli soldiers.

And then there is the Wall itself – eight metres high, a series of huge upended concrete blocks side by side like a giant Lego, which winds up and down the hills and valleys dividing streets, crossing roads, splitting the campus of a University in two, again preventing farmers reaching their fields or their markets, parents seeing their children, and communities meeting each other. All the Palestinians we spoke to seemed to agree that the idea behind its construction was not only to improve security (amazingly, it seems it is not impossible to climb over it) but to destroy the Palestinian economy and social life and culture. One Palestinian house we saw is entirely surrounded by the Wall and Fence and can only be approached by a locked gate.

In the meanwhile, in Arab East Jerusalem, which the Palestinians want as their future capital, their houses are constantly being demolished. The area we saw looked like a war zone littered with ruined houses still full of furniture and household objects. The excuse for this is an Israeli rule that no new building can take place on their land without a permit, the price for which is far beyond the capacity of Palestinians, with their very low wages, to pay. In desperation, they build without one. Then Israeli officials arrive and say the house will be demolished within the next two years, and some time during this period arrive without any further warning, order the householders out of the building in 15 minutes, and then bulldoze it down with anything that has not been removed from it. We met one man who had had three houses destroyed in this way.

"I know they will come back and destroy this one too," he said, "but I shall never leave."

I have since heard a further 88 houses are to be demolished and the whole area is to become a park. It is clear the land grab, far from stopping, is continuing relentlessly. A huge new settlement covering what is now empty land between the north and the south of the West Bank at its narrowest point is to be built and will permanently divide the land.

The reaction of all the other people on this visit was the same: "I had no idea conditions were as bad as this." Nor, we were told by the few clear-sighted Israelis we met, did most Israelis. Their press never speaks of what is going on, very few Israelis visit the territories, and the majority of them are convinced that, as one student put it, "We don't do bad things, the Palestinians are the Baddies, we are the Good People."

But "I only speak what I do know" and, having started from a position of ignorance or even perhaps mild hostility to the Palestinians, I have come to believe the conditions under which they now live are intolerable, unjust, and could never be accepted by any reasonable person.

In previous times the Israelis always demanded a one-state solution to the problem, but this will soon mean they will become a minority of the population and, understandably with their history, they will never agree to this. So now they favour two states. But the state of Palestine they envisage will be one of a series of sealed Bantustans connected to other similar areas by special roads linked by underground tunnels with gates controlled by the IDF. There will be almost no contact with the outside world except to Israeli factories planned to be built nearby, for which they will be a source of cheap labour. Many maps of this proposal are available. Such an arrangement would in no way resemble the viable and contiguous state the Palestinians demand and the world appears to expect.

So the Israelis are faced with a dilemma. In a mirror image of their own history, they want to live in the land of Israel/Palestine without the physical presence of the Palestinians. The only hope left to them appears to be so to harass, oppress and demoralise the Palestinians and destroy their culture, so that eventually they will leave. But if the Palestinians refuse to be ethnically cleansed in this way, there will be violence and bloodshed in the area for the foreseeable future, probably for many centuries. There is almost no time left before this impasse becomes irrevocable.